GEN Z

in the

Workforce

GO BEYOND GEN Z
STEREOTYPES AND BUILD
TOMORROW'S LEADERS

KAT WALSH

ISBN 13: 979-8-9920774-6-9
Library of Congress Catalog Number: 2025920473
First Printing: 2025

Cover design by Emily Mahon
Interior design by Dan Pitts
Edited by Kerry Stapley and Shari MacDonald Strong
Proofread by Abbie Phelps and Quinton Singer
Production editing by Lindsay Bohls and Christine Zuchora-Walske

WISE INK
Wise Ink
PO Box 580195
Minneapolis, MN 55458-0195
wiseink.com

Wise Ink is a creative publishing agency for game-changers. Wise Ink authors uplift, inspire, and inform, and their titles support building a better and more equitable world. For more information, visit wiseink.com.

TABLE OF CONTENTS

PREFACE

For decades I have focused on innovation, placing the customer at the forefront of each business, product/service introduction, or role I've worked.

In 1993, I founded The Monthly Gourmet, the first subscription-model, direct-to-consumer, mail-order meal kit business. The business's function was to facilitate would-be chefs making the complicated recipes they found in the cooking magazines that served as their main source for discovering new recipes. The recipes commonly called for ingredients that weren't available at mainstream grocery stores at the time, and cooks couldn't find the ingredients or make the recipes. I solved the customers' problem by shipping all of the shelf-stable ingredients—especially the specialty and hard-to-find ingredients—they needed to make a gourmet meal, along with several recipes and ideas for decor and music. Essentially, The Monthly Gourmet was a dinner party in a box.

In 1997, I then saw the need for employees to have more options to help them stay mentally and physically healthy, so I founded the Barefoot Scorpion, a business that focused on providing yoga as a service to corporations as part of their employees' benefits plans. At the time, yoga was a relatively uncommon way for people to pursue fitness and well-being. But the employee customers embraced the offering in droves and learned to practice the discipline regularly.

Over the next two decades, I focused on other entrepreneurs who had great ideas. I mentored, funded, and advised young professionals and aspiring entrepreneurs on their new inspirations and businesses. I have helped hundreds of young people think through their business strategies and find success in their start-ups.

In 2020, a unique opportunity presented itself—one that aggregated all of my entrepreneurial experiences with my passion for helping young people find success in life. I was offered the role of chief legacy officer, supporting an ultra-high-net-worth (UHNW) entrepreneur and his family. This role brought together the innovative, tactical, and practical sides of building and executing strategies. Each member of the family already had an individual legacy roadmap designed to empower them to leave their personal mark as well as a plan for how they would become an important contributor to the family legacy.

As the first person to serve this family in a role of this nature, it was up to me to build the methodology and execute the plans that would deliver optimal results for the members of its four living generations. I found members of Generation Z to be the most focused on aligning their careers and lifestyles with their purpose, values, and ideals. They were adamant about incorporating the traditions and knowledge of their upbringing with their youthful sensibilities.

My career path, together with my personal life journey, has informed my focus on Gen Z and on developing their careers. Again today, just as I did with The Monthly Gourmet and the Barefoot Scorpion, I am building an innovative approach to business: focusing on what the customer wants. In this case, the customers are Gen Z employees. I'm focusing on what the Gen Z contributor wants in their career and life. In my work, I have unfolded the map and drawn new routes that help organizations accommodate Gen Z while improving profitability.

By increasing efficiencies along a full spectrum of activities, from efforts to attract candidates through the end of a candidate's employee lifecycle, the human resource (HR) departments that I have helped are achieving a 2.5–3.5 return on their HR investment.

MY FIRST GEN Z RELATIONSHIP: MY PASSION FOR PEOPLE AND PURPOSE

I'm enamored by people who cherish and celebrate their uniqueness and who live authentically. I've learned that these people are the happiest and the most accomplished, live with the greatest intention, and earn their personal legacies.

These special people possess more energy, produce optimal results in their chosen areas of focus, have the most robust relationships, and show high levels of empathy and emotional intelligence. They can be found in all professions, trades, nonprofits, and families. They are quickest to share their non-tangible gifts to encourage success in others.

I have tracked my passion for these types of people and my love of development and high achievement back to my childhood and, in fact, even further than that. My father, the youngest of five children of a single mom, quit school and joined the army to ensure he would have three square meals daily. He had few choices and no formal education, but he had an insatiable curiosity and a mechanically inclined mind. He was what I call a garage genius.

After the army, he married and became a construction worker by trade. He built a reputation as an honest hard worker people wanted to hire. His business thrived because of his strong work ethic, creative problem-solving, and exceptionally high-quality work. He was determined to have summers off in a field in which work done during peak summer hours paid the bills. This meant that he made sacrifices, working eight to nine months of every year without seeing his family much, frequently missing out on holidays, special events, celebrations, and daily hugs.

However, during the summers, he would take my mom and all four of us kids to live on a boat and explore Southeast Alaska for three to four months. I continue to be in awe of my parents for having the courage to transplant our family of six every year for months at a time so they could live out their dreams. They couldn't have known the education I would receive or how it would inform the rest of my life. My parents were the first people I knew to put life ahead of work.

I learned the resilience required to adjust to walking on a boat and then to stand up straight and walk on solid ground again upon mooring. I discovered that the best building in any small village is the library, where people from all walks of life gather to share knowledge and experiences. I know that seafood that is caught, cleaned, and cooked on a tiny stove or beach fire within minutes doesn't need seasonings. I can sleep while the sun is still out, enjoy a hike in the rain, and slow down to look at critters. I believe that nature smells invigorating, sounds serene, tastes traditional, feels textured, and looks pure. Such lessons in resilience, quality, diversity, flexibility, and awareness all remain integral elements of my career focus and the work I do with Gen Z.

The lessons that wriggled deepest into my heart and soul, however, are those that came from the rich knowledge of my Indigenous friends. My Tlingit and Haida friends will be horrified that I refer to them as knowledge keepers in this book, but to me that's what they are. They were my teachers, mentors, and heroes. Their art, stories, music, astronomy, totems, traditions, food, and hunting and fishing skills have informed my head, my heart, and my career.

My First Nations friends respect their heritage and honor their personal journeys through life to an extent I have rarely seen in others. Their purpose in life is not to rush to an end result, but rather to embrace the process, acknowledge and appreciate ancient and new techniques, and reflect daily upon what will bring them closer to their best outcomes. These are all key principles in the process of personal growth and development. I credit my Indigenous teachers for informing my work with these principles.

I also had other teachers in Alaska whose homes I couldn't reach by walking, driving, or taking a bus or train. I had to visit these friends by boat and could do so only when the weather would permit and my parents had it on the agenda. These friends lived off the grid, with what most might consider very little in terms of possessions, but they always had an abundance of hugs, laughter, knowledge, wisdom, and other extraordinary nonfinancial gifts to share with me. From these teachers, I learned that subjective well-being (SWB) is crucial for development and performance.

I had one more important teacher: a locomotive. High in the bush of Southeast Alaska, tucked away in the Berners Bay mining outpost, was an old logging locomotive that had become overgrown by lichen, moss, trees, animal dens, and rust. That little steam locomotive, originally built to bring trees to the bustling economy of the lower forty-eight, would become my teacher and my dad's route to purpose, subjective well-being, and personal growth.

It all began when we took a nearly vertical hike that few people before us had been inclined to try. That day, Dad discovered the historical abandoned equipment that immediately captivated his mechanically inclined mind. Determined to rescue history and feed his thirst for building engines, Dad embarked on an epic project. He salvaged the antique steam locomotive piece by rusty piece, each one shipped first by helicopter out of the bush, then by barge across the Alaskan seaway to Seattle, and finally by train and truck to his property in Northern Nevada.

He rebuilt, restored, and breathed steamy life into the little 1892 H. K. Porter steam locomotive. His work displayed such a high level of perfection that representatives from groups like the Disney Company and the Smithsonian Institute regularly knocked on our door to see the tiny but mighty engine run on its track around his property. My dad became a legend in the niche steam engine space. More than a decade after his death, people still reach out to me to visit his property and see the train run.

My dad and his locomotive taught me the value of focusing on what brings joy and purpose to life. The steam engine has little financial value today, despite the countless hours of work Dad devoted to its restoration. But it was never about money for my dad. The locomotive brought joy to thousands of people during his life and continues to do so. My dad was highly deliberate in how he lived, focused on what made him healthy in heart, mind, and soul. Through the work that many have described as his "legacy," he inspired, and continues to inspire, many current and future engineers and historians.

My Indigenous friends, my dad, and my locomotive teacher have informed my career and this book. From them, I learned respect for a diversity of people, and I learned the importance of traditions and heritage, of living authentically, and of supporting the hopes and dreams of others.

I also learned that invisible, nonfinancial, and non-tangible attributes never diminish in value, have no expiration date, and are not diluted or weakened if spread to many people, and that sharing them improves a person's personal and professional lives.

Incredibly, the more you share your non-tangible, nonfinancial gifts, the greater your mental, physical, and emotional well-being, the stronger your relationships, and the more fulfilling your career.

I feel eternally grateful for my summers spent boating on the Clarence and Chatham Straits, ducking into the little tributaries, bays, inlets, and coves along the winding water pathways. The water was clear, the air was fresh, and the world was majestic. My Alaskan summers taught me to be observant and curious, to explore broadly, and to take thoughtful risks. These are just a few of the lessons I hope to share with you in this book.

INVISIBLE ATTRIBUTES

Attributes, I have learned, when mapped to specific roles, empower individuals and develop successful business leaders, high-performing contributors, and respected managers. While some attributes are innate traits, others are learned, earned, and honed over years of living. Some are generations in the making, born of lessons learned from family heritage and traditions.

Some attributes are underappreciated and have become diluted over the years of living in a society that has worked to homogenize our population. It's shameful that we have become increasingly culturally homogenized, losing many of the learnings taught by our greatest teachers: our ancestors. From European colonialism through the Industrial Revolution, imperialism, post-war Reconstruction, the Civil Rights Movement, the technology revolution, and globalization, we have with each new decade either forced others or chosen ourselves to become more removed from the traditions and heritage we once valued so highly.

For decades, our society's behavior has been characterized by the phrase "keeping up with the Joneses," a concept deeply rooted in conformity and financial competition rather than in human values. In fact, the boomer generation is often referred to as Generation Jones for those reasons. However, Gen Z is animated about individuality and celebrating uniqueness. They increasingly focus on living a life based on individual preferences and lifestyle choices rather than on keeping up with the Joneses.

This book is about hyper-individualization: finding and focusing upon the specific qualities each person needs to feel fully satisfied in life and in their career. For the first time since the term "having it all" became popular in the 1980s, Gen Z may be the generation that achieves a balance of career, family, and personal well-being.

Incredibly, my dad was one of the early adopters of what is now considered part of a Gen Z movement: life–work balance. You will see throughout this book that life–work balance represents a fundamental change in how many contributors evaluate success. In my life, I saw that my dad developed a hyper-individualized plan for himself that aligned with his career, life purpose, beliefs, and lifestyle. While most of his generation was bound to a work–life balance, my dad chose the life–work balance, prioritizing lifestyle, personal growth, and the well-being of his family above all else.

This didn't happen for my dad without a detailed plan that he, my mom, and my siblings and I lived by, day in and day out. The same is true for employee contributors who want to live a specific life: They need a plan and devotion to its execution. With a plan, focused execution, and ongoing effort, individuals and their organizations can achieve well-being, success, and long-term relationships with each other.

WHY SHOULD YOU CARE ABOUT GEN Z?

The population seems to be split on the importance of discussing Gen Z in the workforce. For some people, the "who cares" philosophy roughly translates to "I'm not concerned about Gen Z; they'll come along when they get hungry enough." And then there are the I-carers, whose philosophy is essentially "We need a workforce to continue to thrive in our business; we have an opportunity to learn and teach our next generation of leaders."

I fall into the second category, and this book has been written to help explain Gen Z's thinking. I have researched deeply to understand why they behave the way they do. I have also helped businesses and business leaders to innovate their talent acquisition and retention processes in order to attract, interview, hire, onboard, develop, and engage Gen Z.

There are roughly fifty million Gen Z professionals in the workforce, and over half will either leave their jobs or be let go within six months of being hired. The cost of replacing a contributor is estimated to be between one-third and two-thirds of their annual salary, depending on the technical requirements of the role.

With a median annual salary for entry-level contributors at $50,000, the estimated cost to the US economy for replacing Gen Z employees who leave their jobs within the first six months is between $312.5 billion and $937.5 billion annually. For a company with one hundred Gen Z employees, if half leave their jobs, the estimated replacement cost would be between $625,000 and $1,875,000.

That's the payroll and paper cost, the money you see on your balance sheet. But the productivity, morale, and cost to your company's reputation have an exponential impact that can't be fully measured.

By investing in meaningful solutions to address the Gen Z mentality, businesses can reduce turnover and foster a culture that supports long-term retention. Rather than viewing Gen Z's workplace expectations as obstacles, forward-thinking leaders recognize them as opportunities to create a more dynamic, inclusive, and adaptive work environment.

Companies that take the time to understand and align with Gen Z's values—such as flexibility, purpose-driven work, and continuous learning—will reduce costly turnover and build a resilient workforce that's poised for sustained success. The businesses that thrive in the coming decades will be those that bridge generational gaps, embrace innovation in talent management, and invest in the professional growth of their youngest employees.

Ultimately, the choice is clear: Adapt and cultivate Gen Z's potential or risk falling behind in an evolving labor market where the competition for talent is fiercer than ever.

PART
ONE
GENERATION Z

CHAPTER ONE

GEN Z:
UNIQUE AND EXTRAORDINARY

As a lifelong futurist and innovator with a special fondness for boosting subjective well-being and striving to support the unique and individual personalities within humanity, I will help you rethink how you can maximize the impact of Gen Z in your workplace. I'll also explain why doing this is important enough that you should spend your precious time and financial resources to do so.

I'm a Gen Z-ologist. Just as scientists and specialists in other fields devote themselves to studying a particular niche topic, I have dedicated myself to studying Generation Z. The most educated generation in US history, they bring fresh ideas, boundless imagination and innovation, and critical thinking processes into their careers. Yet they are misunderstood and mocked because they think differently than older generations. Simply put, there is a generational bias against Gen Z.

The United States' mission of progress, democracy, individual success, and freedom of thought extends into business. Historically, our country has embraced entrepreneurs who have evolved businesses and boosted political, economic, and cultural systems. I have spent three years researching this book, I live and breathe Gen Z, and I believe that members of that generation are innovators—sometimes disruptive ones, but innovators nonetheless—in the business space.

Gen Z make up no more negative a workforce than did any generation that preceded them and insisted upon new policies and growth. I have researched each generation in the workplace and understand that many who have come before Gen Z have wished for what Gen Z is brave enough to actually ask for.

In my work, I have learned to use every tool available to understand the complexities businesses face as they look forward to the next decade. Through observation, primary research, profound AI-based discovery, interviews, and a systematic, data-driven study of each generation, I have gathered insight and methods to address the complicated issues businesses face. Using the techniques of researchers before me, I surveyed, interviewed, and conducted focus groups of people who provided insight and knowledge. For this book, I have read countless research works written by people across a broad industry base: economists, philosophers, neurologists, psychologists, social anthropologists, wealth planners, and many from the other science fields and human science disciplines.

I've gathered anecdotal insight from professors, parents, employers, Gen Z members, members of previous generations, and casual observers from all walks of life. I've never met a single person who had no opinion or thoughts about people from Gen Z, also known as Zoomers.

I use many quantitative methods of gathering data, conducting experiments, and analyzing results to advance my knowledge and appreciation of Gen Z. However, I am not blind to this particular generation's naivete regarding some aspects of living in the real world, a naivete driven by economic, cultural, and political conditions. It's important to note that the Gen Z mindset I refer to throughout this book is the result of a complex mix of societal factors, educational approaches, and parenting styles. These forces have collectively created a generation that is often bold, opinionated, and confident: traits that many business leaders respect and strive to develop in themselves.

USING UP HUMAN RESOURCES IS KILLING THE WORKFORCE

A *resource* is a stock or supply of money, materials, staff, and other assets that can be drawn on by a person or organization in order to function effectively. No one wants to be an organization's resource that is used, or even worse, used *up*. They want to participate in the success of your organization by contributing an endless supply of talents and abilities. They want to develop and learn so that they can increasingly provide a contribution.

Committed organizations that innovate their HR departments so they can integrate Gen Z will be rewarded. The ideals and mindset the Zoomers bring to the workplace are not going to reverse themselves as the workplace begins to integrate their younger counterparts, Generation Alpha, so the groundwork employers lay today will be useful for many years to come.

Consider what will happen if we don't address the ever-bulging gap between Gen Z and the practicalities of running businesses and maintaining our leadership roles in world economics. In that scenario, we will leave a monumental issue for future generations to address. We will offer our descendants an economy that became unhealthy within one generation of humanity.

Whether or not executives and board members agree with the mindset and attitudes of Gen Z, they need to find a middle ground. The viability and future success of their organizations depend upon this accommodation.

Organizations that learn, teach, lead, and engage their young professional workforce will experience financial rewards. Seamless integration of the next generations of leaders with previous ones is mutually beneficial to all stakeholders of the organization and to the overall brand image of the organization. If this is done well, executives will deliver improved financial results, attract high-caliber talent, provide positive corporate social responsibility messaging, and influence customer loyalty.

Gen Z is also, dare I say, suspicious of unproven or theoretical advice. For that reason, I will provide in this book as much fact-based, human science as I feel is palatable in a book for general readers.

WE HAVE CULPABILITY: WE TAUGHT GEN Z TO BE GEN Z

I want to explain that I'm not one-sided in my views about Gen Z's influence in the workplace. I see at least two sides to every conversation about young professionals and the companies that hire them. I do, however, believe that although a lot of research has been conducted, and although many people are talking about the changes Gen Z is making in the workforce, few are solving for the gap between them and organizations. The fact is, Gen Z will comprise more and more of the workforce as we move through the years, and organizations need to learn to work with them.

And their presence is not just contained to contributors. Over time, they will make up an even greater percentage of customers, managers, business partners, clients, and teammates. The youngest Zoomers will not matriculate into the workforce until 2033, so we have a true, compelling reason to focus on them now. As a futurist, I don't believe ignoring a clear trend is a wise business decision.

As their more-experienced teachers, parents, colleagues, friends, and neighbors from a prior generation, we are culpable for how they act, think, and express themselves. We taught them to be independent thinkers and to not accept things blindly. We encouraged them to develop new, creative solutions and to not be afraid to express their thoughts. All of these behaviors are the very ones people now criticize them for.

Gen Z is innovating human resources and commerce more profoundly, and in a shorter amount of time, than any prior generation has done. We can either learn from them, teach them, and collaborate with them, or we can allow our economy to suffer without them.

LAUREN'S STORY

Lauren had been talking to her team for years about an inevitable development: The hiring space is changing, and those changes will continue to cause challenges. Her company had been a "Best Places to Work" A-lister for decades, partly because of its focus on benefits. Her organization offered best-in-class compensation and health care. Yet in recent years, she and her chief executive officer (CEO) had begun to have new conversations about preparing for technological advancements while also promoting what Lauren was beginning to notice was an appreciation for heritage and lifestyle among job candidates.

A thirty-year veteran of human resources and an early adopter of new HR technology throughout her career, Lauren had begun in the last decade to see significant changes in specific key performance indicators (KPIs) that seemed to reflect a changing focus from compensation to nontraditional, values-based benefits. She said that she noticed "many of the same things my colleagues in HR were seeing at their organizations: an inverse relationship between application turn-in rates and offer acceptance rates."

She was concerned. There was an increase in applications, but those applications weren't converting to new hires. Since she had adopted online application software in the early 2000s, she'd seen an ever-increasing number of applications for each job posting but a negative trend in her application-to-hire ratio.

Lauren began to vigilantly track and analyze the questions her teams were fielding in their candidate screenings and phone interviews. Particularly noticeable to her, beginning in 2019, were the candidates' questions about the company's corporate social responsibility and environmental, social, and governance commitments. She was also intrigued by the increasing number of questions about family planning, time off, flexible work, and mental health. "More young people want to work from home and ask about vacation time than any other generation before them," she said. She explains that candidates don't wait for an offer; they ask for one in the first two conversations.

In prior years, she had fielded questions about company matching programs, 401(k)s, stock options, and employer-sponsored health care; questions about lifestyle and the balance of career and life were now replacing those. If an entry-level candidate gets to the offer, she says, "They don't negotiate for anything other than annual salary and time off; other traditional compensation requests don't come up like they used to." Gen Z, she noticed, view traditional benefits as table stakes and focus instead on new categories of benefits in their negotiations.

Regarding salary, young professionals value their take-home amount more than they do their investment compensation. This change in attitude aligns with their belief that they want personal control, which they see reflected in an ability to make their own decisions about how and where they spend or invest their money.

Other important KPIs were also changing. Lauren's job postings had produced fewer qualified candidates. New hires were staying at the organization for an average of six months, and many left before onboarding was complete.

Lauren's organization subsequently embarked on an end-to-end program I designed for the company that focused upon attracting, hiring, onboarding, developing, and engaging Gen Z, as well as earning their loyalty and improving their performance. As a result, Lauren's retention of entry-level contributors went from six months to two years. This is the same methodology that this book will teach you to implement.

> **Best Practice: Gen Z is committed to development, so focus your organization on an end-to-end contributor experience in order to elicit loyal Gen Z performance.**

MING'S STORY

Ming, the chairman and CEO of a start-up, had experienced decades of success with prior start-ups and public organizations in the pharmaceutics sector, yet he began to notice recruiting complexities in recent years. His business, which relied upon highly technical, science-educated research talent, had begun to see a decline in qualified candidates. While he'd already been constrained by the number of students who specialize in the specific area of research he requires, he now found that even fewer young people were willing to dedicate themselves to a discipline whose job market outlook was uncertain. They began to obtain the minimum science requirement and double major in business as a fallback career path rather than committing to the field with the vigor that had been demonstrated by prior research students.

The sources he'd historically used to recruit for his organizations no longer provided the number of scientists his industry needed, and his start-up company couldn't provide the same financial and health benefits large public companies could provide. However, his nimble organization offered different benefits than large pharmaceutical companies, such as a higher individual contribution to R & D projects, more interaction with leadership, and a potential ownership stake.

As an adjunct professor at a large public university renowned for producing top-level researchers, Ming also saw a significant recent change from his teaching perspective: Fewer students were entering his department's program for the purpose of conducting research. Instead, they planned to join consulting firms that paid better and provided more predictable benefits, particularly paid time off, or start-ups that offered a partnership stake in the business.

Drawing on Ming's knowledge of students and young professionals, he and I worked together to redesign his start-up's benefits offering, adding a week off during the last week of December. He also created a scholarship that included an interview and job preparation program for students who met a specific academic standard. Essentially, Ming helped the scholarship's recipients pay for their education and provided them with the comfort of knowing they would be trained to secure a job. With these two changes, Ming earned the trust of his students, and he was able to attract 30 percent more researchers to his firm upon graduation. And still, many would not commit to the program.

The results increased our curiosity and gave us more questions to ask:

1. If they were offered a role in the field they were going to college to study, why wouldn't they commit to an offer that was standard in the industry within their narrow field of research?

2. Why did some students feel neutral about accepting the offer when their stated goals were to work in this industry?
3. What value did they place on the additional week of paid time off and on the training on how to interview?

We interviewed the students who were willing to share details to help Ming's program; some of their language is quoted here. According to the students, they "expected" two weeks off; an additional week was nice but not that "earth-shattering." Standard compensation and health care benefits were expected, but they were not enough to entice the students to commit to the role.

The most appealing incentive to the students was the interview and job preparation program. The students felt that Ming "cared" and was "looking out for [their] best interests, not just his own." They felt they lacked the social and leadership skills to appeal to an interviewer, so they appreciated learning those skills before they needed to use them.

In addition to the interview questions, we asked the students, "What would you like to see added to the benefits to boost your odds of accepting the role?" First, the students wanted more time off, to be taken at their discretion, not when the company told them to take it.

Secondly, they wanted to improve their business knowledge without committing to a full major or minor in business while earning their degree. They felt that business knowledge would result in more opportunities in R & D. The students felt confident that learning how to commercialize—the process behind product development—and how to manage people would give them options upon graduation. Their responses indicated their interest in contributing at their highest level of potential and learning the business side of research and development; they wanted to be in research and be financially successful.

Gen Z wants to be well-rounded in order to have the most career options. To meet this need, focus your organization on providing education and training in areas that align with workers' future ambitions and directly support their roles.

Ming and I conducted a directional study to inform his benefits package. This study informs us about the logic this group of young, highly educated technical thinkers uses when considering their futures. As business leaders can attest, no one can ever honorably promise what the future will offer. Still, leaders who understand their specific Gen Z population will find they have loyal Gen Z contributors.

In Ming's case, Gen Z workers were more focused on options than on a potential benefit that might never come to fruition. Many students at this age live with stars in their eyes and hopes and dreams about their futures. They have fantastic aspirations, but they also know that most people don't achieve fame, particularly in the field of research, where millions of brilliant scientists toil for a lifetime without making the "big discovery" that earns them a Nobel Prize. For this reason, they feel better with a backup plan: knowledge of business to support their research degrees.

Young professionals today will gladly vocalize their ambitions and requests. Earlier generations put their heads down and humbly worked for decades to fulfill their dreams. Gen Z strives for more predictability and isn't afraid to ask for it.

Through this program, Ming and I learned that the key to attracting the best talent for his business was being clear, honest, and generous in offering support for workers' futures, as well as being specific about the realities of working in the research field.

CHAPTER TWO

GENERATIONAL BIAS

Your company doesn't need to start a full-scale Gen Z revolution in your workplace. Small steps lead to excellent organization-wide outcomes. The first step is to remove generational biases; bring generations together to appreciate one another and leverage their combined strengths.

Every generation seems to be annoyed and confused by other generations. "These young people don't" or "The older people don't" is muttered as a lead-in to endless complaints about how other generations think and behave. Generational bias goes both ways, up and down the ages, with people from all age groups judging others' behaviors and ideas.

Bias creates misunderstandings and conflicts. Throughout history, people have judged others without attempting to understand why they behave the way they do, and this continues in modern times. While it's impossible to characterize an entire generation by their behaviors and philosophies, some world events shape tendencies and sensibilities among larger groups of people.

THE GENERATIONS

There is no formal authority that designates the years of each generation. For that reason, you'll run across books and articles that define the generations using different birth years. In this book, I use the following table and birth years.

GENERATIONS TABLE

1901–1924	1925–1945	1946–1964	1965–1980	1981–1996	1997–2012	2013–2025
THE GREATEST GEN	THE SILENT GEN	THE BOOMERS	GEN X	GEN Y OR MILLENNIALS	GEN Z	GEN ALPHA

Because each person has a unique life experience that informs their values, beliefs, character, morals, perceptions, ideas, abilities, and so on, it is impossible to write a story that is true for all members of a generation. I also cannot slot people perfectly into one generation or another. Instead, people almost always have characteristics that cross many or all generations.

Yet world events and economics, parenting and business management styles, and cultural influences all inform spending habits, lifestyle choices, work ethics, and many other behaviors that can describe a larger group of people—a generation of people.

To indicate why each generation has distinct social and work sensibilities, a brief explanation of the generations follows. My intention is not to write an exhaustive study of the generations but rather to provide a quick reference to the lives and influences for each of the generations that follow.

While techniques and behaviors changed over the decades, one thing has always been consistent: Each generation was doing what they believed would help their children succeed.

The Greatest and Silent Generations: The Boss Leader

Members of the Greatest Generation and the Silent Generation came of age during some of the most challenging world events in modern history: WWI, WWII, and the Great Depression. These world events drove increased unemployment, poverty, and a sense of uncertainty. These tough times taught people to survive on little, and to value hard work, grit, thriftiness, and community spirit.

Due to a scarcity of leisure time in which to "explore options" for work, as future generations would do, members of these generations respected a direct, almost militant, style of leadership. They wanted a confident leader who told them exactly what to do, and they would put their heads down and get the job done without asking questions.

They called these leaders "the boss." There was a clear hierarchy and respect for leadership. At home, these men raised their children in much the same way, telling their children what they needed to get done and expecting them to do it without question. Essentially, they became the bosses of their homes.

While the world wars shaped the solemn characters of the men and women who served, their loved ones who supported the war effort from home also learned to be stoic and hardworking. They had to pick up the slack because their military family members could no longer help.

In parenting, terms like "Because I said so" and "Don't ask why; I have my reasons" were commonplace. There was an unquestioning reverence for rank. But these terms would eventually result in annoyed children rather than motivated ones.

As parenting evolved, phrases like those would be replaced by increasingly gentle parenting approaches and communications that would inform, both positively and negatively, how each progressive generation accepted hierarchy and responded to commands, both at home and in the workplace.

The Boomer Generation

The children who were taught to "Do as I say" started their lives complying with that directive. They grew up during a time when blending into society was respected. Legal immigrants didn't want to stand out; they wanted to go unnoticed. They tried to create the "perfect family" as depicted on television programs of the time, such as *The Adventures of Ozzie and Harriet, My Three Sons, Leave It to Beaver,* and other shows that portrayed how a "respectable" family should behave.

Yet as the boomers came of age, they experienced life through tragic events like the unrest of the Civil Rights Movement, the assassinations of prominent leaders like Martin Luther King Jr. and President Kennedy, and the Vietnam War draft. They began to separate themselves from conflict and gave birth to the counterculture movement: peace, love, and communal living. They became known as the hippies.

Whereas their parents had suffered financial hardships, the boomers began to trade in their hippie lifestyle during the work week, ushering in Generation Jones and pushing one another toward economic excellence, represented by money in the bank and a white picket fence. They succeeded to an extraordinary level and are expected to leave a collective inheritance of $73 trillion to their descendants, which will shape future generations' behaviors and attitudes.

The boomers wanted their children, Generation X, to succeed by new standards: college education and careers. Even if they weren't boys! This shift marks the determination of women from this generation to become college educated and to join the workforce in the same way their siblings and fathers had done.

Generation X

Men and women began to focus on their career success as measured by job title and by the respect, prestige, and money that came along with it. They worked endlessly to climb the corporate ladder and "have it all": a career, a family, a committed relationship, and personal growth. It is widely recognized that few men, and even fewer women, succeeded in this quest; *Harvard Business Review* proclaims "the painful truth is that women in the United States don't 'have it all.'"[1] But the ambition was present nonetheless.

There were many roadblocks to women having it all, many involving the ways they were stereotyped as wives, housemakers, and mothers. Unwritten customs and policies discriminated against women, particularly those considered to be of marriageable or childbearing ages. It was assumed that these women would be unable to manage their workload when they became distracted by love. People thought that women would prioritize life over careers. For that reason, many roles and promotions were reserved for the men, who managers assumed were less dedicated to their families and home life.

This focus on climbing the ladder led to the emergence of servant leaders who put others before themselves. The servant leader inserted more management levels into the corporate ladder to accommodate the Gen X quest for a respected title. The idea was that if there were more rungs on the ladder, more people could climb simultaneously.

MORE RUNGS ON THE LADDER

---

1   Sylvia Ann Hewlett, "Executive Women and the Myth of Having It All," *Harvard Business Review*, April 2002, https://hbr.org/2002/04/executive-women-and-the-myth-of-having-it-all.

These additional levels of management created top-heavy organizations that some are now working to flatten in the present workplace. The focus upon title and long work hours over strict meritocracy in performance has also created a conflict between generations. Older generations insist upon being granted the respect they feel they have earned by climbing the ladder, while Gen Z insist that title is less important than are money and development in the workplace.

Generation X began to raise their children with a focus on inclusion, participation, and emotional well-being, instead of on winning. Many of them had not won the ultimate prize of "having it all," and they taught their children that it was not necessary to win, but that it was important to participate.

The Millennials or Gen Y

With their parents' encouragement to prioritize mental well-being, many millennials shifted their focus toward experiences rather than material possessions. They began investing in experiences and conveniences that freed up time and allowed them to enjoy even more meaningful experiences.

Traditional career success is still a primary focus for millennials, and for some, the financial stability they have inherited plays a role in their ability to focus on passion and experiences over income. Others who didn't inherit wealth have rejected the idea of money as a be-all and end-all worth the sacrifice of not being home with loved ones and not living a passionate life.

The Gen Z Movement

That brings us to Gen Z: the focus of many executives, managers, and workforce contributors. The fact that this generation representing sixty-nine million US citizens is seen as something of a caricature is surprising, and this misrepresentation is based on the very labels that other generations tie to them: blind belief in misleading information and social media hoopla.

There have been many movements throughout history: labor, women's suffrage, Prohibition, antinuclear, LGBTQ+ rights, Indigenous rights, and many, many others. The Gen Z movement is different because it cannot be tethered to a singular mission, purpose, or outcome. It's not possible to say "if this, then that" with Gen Z, as you can with other movements, as in the following example from women's suffrage: "If we earn the right to vote, we will stop marching."

Instead, the Gen Z movement is a prismatic, shapeless ideology that has no bounds or constraints. It can't be measured or restrained, yet it is a refined philosophy with a common theme: personal values, purpose, and lifestyle choices are collectively the most important part of life.

Because business has traditionally been built upon systematic processes and efficiencies, trying to comply with Gen Z's numerous individual goals has caused strife among business leaders. For that reason, some business leaders are saying "They'll come around when they're hungry" and ignoring the movement. As a futurist and as a businessperson, I don't think it's a good idea to ignore a clear change in the way the next generation of workers thinks. Instead, business leaders have an opportunity to recognize this change, plan for it, and use that plan to outperform those who don't address it.

The biggest change in individual contributor support and development is enabled by technological advancements. We can provide hyper-individualized training programs that build high-performing young professionals who become increasingly productive leaders. Leaders who remove generational biases and take advantage of technology to gather information and design programs for their young contributors will see loyal, productive successors emerge.

As organizations continue to remove unnecessary layers of management, becoming increasingly decentralized and collaborative, there will be more interaction and necessary communications between leadership and individual contributors throughout the organization. Leaders who know how to interpret Gen Z language and draw meaning from it will succeed and find themselves set apart from those who wait for the inevitable changing of the guard.

Organizations that have the appetite to dive into the tendencies and sensibilities of Gen Z, and that seek to understand them fully, will have a robust young professional workforce that works with them, not against them.

In this book, I hope to dispel the mystery that surrounds a generation of bold, innovative, and ambitious young next-generation leaders. While their stated purpose in life may differ from that of older generations, having a new perspective always brings about thought-provoking change. Change is what built our country and our businesses.

COMPARING GENERATIONS

	Boomers	Gen X	Millennials	Gen Z
Life Focus	Security; Basic Needs	Buying Vacation Homes; Building Wealth; Career Titles	Experiences and Conveniences	Having Purpose; Prioritizing Lifestyle and Balance
Effective Manager Style	Controls the workplace with authority; No questions asked.	Directs workforce with confidence and earned respect. Contributors question little about a leader's rationale.	Manages with strong guidance; Collaboration becomes more important.	Leads with collaborative style that allows ownership and empowerment.

Each generation wants more ownership, collaboration, and flexibility.

WHAT CHANGED?

Every generation has acknowledged a chasm between parents and their children with regard to what is considered appropriate and respectable. Parents of the '60s thought they had the answers to how people should dress, live, work, and play. Their children disagreed; they became "rebels," rejecting societal norms, pursuing alternative lifestyles, abandoning traditional career paths for alternative ways of living, and questioning authority.

In recent years, those same cultural and lifestyle upheavals have occurred again. This time, however, instead of rebelling against their parents, Gen Z are doing what their parents and the education system have unwittingly guided them to do. Members of earlier generations were expected to unquestioningly respect elders and to do what doctors, lawyers, teachers, religious leaders, and parents said to do, without questioning them. Those children, now parents, went on to encourage their Gen Z offspring to ask questions and forge new pathways.

Concerning work, Gen Z saw their parents accept jobs as they were instead of challenging anything about them. I noticed that disheartening trend of apathy and resignation from inside my first corporate role. On day three at the public company where I worked, I met Sally, a boomer with a tenure of twenty years. She smiled big, laughed readily, and knew everyone in the building.

That day, Sally invited me to lunch. I couldn't wait to learn everything I could about her, the company, and how to excel in my role. We sat down, and immediately Sally told me she had eleven years until her retirement. I smiled, but I remember feeling a mixture of disgust, sickness, and sadness as my internal voice screamed, *I never want to be counting a single year of my life away.*

While prior generations were often rebels outside of work, they conformed and made no waves in their jobs. For generations, many people built their lives, as Sally had, around their careers, showing loyalty to their employer until retirement. Their careers determined their level of happiness, where they lived, and how they socialized; even children's births had to fit around work schedules. But many of these people, also like Sally, were not motivated, engaged, or enthused about work—it was simply a means to an end.

Eventually, as work hours extended and individual expectations increased, balancing a family, career, and social life became increasingly difficult. It became more and more challenging to find a work–life balance.

Boomers and Gen Xers struggled to find a tolerable level of peace outside of work because they were focused on getting ahead.

Many people struggled to balance work and life and resigned themselves to counting the years until retirement, as Sally did. Realizing they couldn't change their circumstances, they accepted their situation and focused on looking forward to life *after retirement.* This attitude was so common that many could recite their exact retirement date, down to the day, years in advance.

Then, the COVID-19 pandemic hit, and contributors got a taste of working from home. They experienced a life in which commutes lasted five minutes or less; they discovered they had time for their families and hobbies. This event accelerated the inevitable: a reset of work–life balance. No longer would careers dictate family, lifestyle, and personal growth. Today, more people want a lifestyle that informs a career. In pursuit of that goal, the US workforce continues to flip from work–life balance to life–work balance. Life comes first.

Life–work balance may be a phenomenon associated with young professionals, but people across generations have experienced positive emotional benefits from having extra time, even extra days, in their after-hours lives. They have embraced the chance to spend their time doing whatever makes them happiest, instead of commuting, traveling, or going to conferences.

Individual Values Replace Corporate Values

Throughout my life, when I've been interviewing for various roles, it has not been uncommon for me to be asked to recite the company's mission statement and to be quizzed on it and on the underlying organizational values I am to live by. I have walked through countless warehouses, manufacturing plants, and headquarters where I saw framed quotes outlining the organization's value statements. None of those calligraphed phrases was inherently bad, but many of them needed to be more compelling. They reminded me of the wisdom I got in a quote-of-the-day calendar. The memorization and recitation of them was simply a means to an end: getting a job.

Gen Z is different. Instead of joining and staying at companies that ask them to recite the company mission and values, they want their employers' mission statements to reflect the values they stand for, their beliefs, and the contributions they want to make to the company and the world. They want their employer to help them develop career plans that celebrate their individuality and unique thinking, and that support their values and goals. To be clear, they aren't asking anyone else to change their values systems—they are, however, searching for organizations that align with the ones they hold.

When organizational values and the values of a member of Gen Z align, the organization will benefit by building an engaged, loyal leader. In turn, these engaged contributors will create new customer bases and socialize their organization's value, ultimately impacting the organization's financial outcomes.

> Gen Z wants to work for a company whose mission is "Value Our Contributors' Values and Missions," not the reverse.

Corporate leaders and human resources teams are uniquely positioned to improve the emotional, physical, and mental well-being of their Gen Z contributors. By doing so, they will lead motivated, upbeat high performers that remain with organizations, lowering the operational costs of attracting, hiring, onboarding, developing, and engaging young professionals.

Please don't mistake my appreciation of Gen Z as my agreement with everything they stand for and ask for. Gen Z has a lot of learning and experience to gain. Many Gen Z workers have yet to run a successful business, plan for retirement, raise a family, experience a stock market crash that impacts their bank account, or navigate countless other life challenges. Yet I understand that their underlying quest is to live their best life, and I applaud their mission.

Gen Z's Number One Goal: Life–Work Balance

Historically, an individual's career dictated where they lived, how they socialized, when they started and built a family, and how much time they had for personal, spiritual, and social development. For generations, people have built their lives around their careers. Emphasizing work above all else was considered the cost of having a robust career.

Having a laser focus on career was respected and admired. Eventually, society termed the act of aligning every aspect of life with the demands of a career "finding work–life balance." Work–life balance was the ultimate prize, earned by building a robust career while finding a tolerable level of peace in other areas of life. As the number of women joining the workforce increased, families, marriages, and personal well-being felt the strain.

Career became the focus of many life decisions. Where the family lived depended upon job locations. Job promotions determined where the family relocated. People commuted by plane. Parents missed school performances, events, and family dinners regularly. All to "have it all" and have a "work–life balance."

"Finding work–life balance" became a mantra and goal of countless couples as they fought to have thriving careers, relationships, and families, as well as personal well-being. Conflicting goals arose as some business leaders expected round-the-clock performance from high-level executives, while children unknowingly made equally ardent demands on their parent's time.

Gen Z is turning the work–life balance ideology upside down and prioritizing life. Work–life balance becomes life–work balance

Gen Z believe that their career and lifestyle should enhance each other to build overall well-being and life satisfaction. Gen Z highly value aligning careers with their lifestyle, family, personal growth, relationships, social interactions, and mental well-being. They feel that a job should improve those things, not impede them.

Gen Z take a lot of heat for being vocal and animated about this change in perspective. They are unfairly accused of being lazy, unambitious, entitled, uninformed, and so on. But Zoomers want robust careers and expect to work hard to climb the corporate ladder. They want a career that brings money and fulfillment, but their measure of true success is life.

It is Gen Z's belief that success that puts lifestyle choices at the center of all other decisions makes for the best life. They want to build a thriving career like their parents and grandparents did, but they believe that careers should align with their lifestyle decisions, not dictate them. They elect to first envision where and how they live and then select a job that supports and boosts those decisions.

How Gen Z Became the Life-Work Generation

This generation has experienced turmoil their whole lives. They have been through active shooter drills in their schools, religious institutions, and community centers. Young people from ages twelve to thirty-five tell me that they rarely walk into a theater, ball game, concert, school, or church without considering an escape route in case of an active shooter. The rules for young people have changed in nearly every aspect of their lives—including their careers.

Covid impacted the world and caused disaster and hardships for all people. Because the Gen Z generation was so young at the time, much of the public doesn't appreciate that many of its members had several of their lifelong goals derailed in a matter of months. For some, major, significant coming-of-age events evaporated. Milestone moments, such as graduating from high school or college, starting a first professional job, and achieving financial independence, were abruptly put on hold. After years—sometimes decades—of hard work and planning, the closures and restrictions caused by Covid disrupted dreams and aspirations for Gen Z.

Each year, additional research about mental health in young people shows decreases in mental well-being and increases in anxiety among our Generation Z population; we aren't able to stop the negative momentum. Research shows that over half of Gen Z battles depression and feelings of hopelessness. Almost two-thirds of our young people have professionally diagnosed anxiety.

Unlike their older relations, Gen Z are proactive about getting medical and therapeutic help for their mental health. They are more than twice as likely to seek support for their conditions. They are taking their mental health into their own hands and putting it at the forefront of many other life decisions.

Gen Z's key characteristics have resulted from the world they have survived and have been crucial in establishing their life–work focus. They have learned that life is not always under their control, so where they can have control, they want to. They have learned that external influences can create anxiety and emotional strain. Because they are determined to boost their mental health, they put life before work and strive for a life–work balance.

A Gen Z life–work philosophy: Much of life is out of my control, and anything can happen— live for the moment and focus on emotional, physical, and mental well-being.

In the late part of the century, young people learned to think independently, challenge ideas, develop innovative solutions to problems, and trust their voices and thinking. They were encouraged to gather intelligence but make their own decisions. Society applauded them for dreaming big and "making things happen."

At this time, the children of those "make things happen" workers saw their parents burn out; take two weeks of vacation spread out over fifty-two weeks of the year; work while ill; travel five days a week, missing games, recitals, and parties for work events; and watch the clock for the end of each work day. Parents came home mentally and physically exhausted, unable to engage fully with their loved ones. In the last half of the twentieth century, a person often achieved career success by sacrificing their well-being.

Gen Z are determined to have a family or chosen community, maintain mental and physical health, live a chosen lifestyle, achieve financial stability, and pursue a career they love. They are committed to a shared support system that encompasses career, lifestyle, and personal health. They understand that a single aspect of life does not define its overall quality.

You can transfer many concepts I've learned from Gen Z to other workforce generations. As more people begin to understand the Gen Z mentality, I hear more and more people admit that Gen Z thinking has merit when it comes to leading and managing young talent and having a well-lived life.

Today, life–work balance is a cross-demographic, cross-ethnicity, cross-gender, and cross-generational collection of goals for finding a lifestyle that aligns personal values and purpose with career, lifestyle choices, family, personal growth, and subjective well-being.

TIME OUT: PTO

Interesting facts about paid time off (PTO) in the United States tell us more about reality. According to *Forbes*, in 2018, Americans on average took 17.4 days of PTO, a slight increase from 2017. Yet twenty-eight million Americans, mostly hourly workers, don't get paid vacations or holidays.

The International Monetary Fund (IMF) uses the term "advanced economy" to describe countries that have high per capita income, diversified industrial and service sectors, and high standards of living. The United States is the only advanced economy in the world that does not guarantee its workers paid vacation days. And 31 percent of hardworking Americans work in roles without PTO for months or even years without any break, lacking the work–life balance that is important for their physical and mental well-being.

Over 50 percent of associates in the older generations say they have worked while on PTO. They check their emails, take calls, or work during their PTO. Gen Z are less likely to continue that trend. Gen Z want to be offered the opportunity to enjoy their time off when they're on PTO. This, they say, contributes to their life–work balance.

CHAPTER THREE

GEN Z MYTHOLOGY

Mythology, in one sense, is simply a collection of ancient stories that cultures have passed down to explain the unknown, like natural events or the origins of humanity. In another sense, mythology can describe the deep systems of belief that shape a society's values. As with all oral storytelling and traditions, in which stories morph and grow, becoming less factual over time, the stories told about Gen Z have become fairy tales, beasts with a tailwind. Many are generalizations that have grown into outsized myths. Indeed, Gen Z's worldview differs from that of older generations, but many stories about them are exaggerated.

Some leaders write Gen Zers off rather than attempting to understand and innovate HR to include them in the workforce. Although many people feel confused about their behavior, understanding their viewpoint is still essential when operating a business that has them as an ever-increasing percentage of the workforce.

It's unproductive to make business decisions based on generalizations about the entire sixty-nine million members of Gen Z.

Today, AI enables a micro-understanding of each individual, removing the group bias about Gen Z that leads to generalizations and misunderstandings. Capital that's spent in HR to understand the individual results in a replacement or augmentation of the manager's bias and opinion-based conclusions about attracting, hiring, onboarding, developing, and engaging their future workforce. Companies will see a return on this AI investment in loyalty, tenure, cultural improvements, and individual performance.

HR capital no longer buys a cohort of talent; HR capital spent on AI identifies the micro-personality of individual contributors to ensure that a highly compatible contributor fills each open role.

The general population describes Gen Z as being entitled, superficial, unambitious, disloyal, and internally focused, and as having short attention spans and poor communication skills. One shared demographic, such as age range, does not provide a basis for accurately describing all members of that population. Members of each generation certainly have similar tendencies that are based on world influences and economics. Still, the success of integrating Gen Z into the workforce depends upon HR's ability to recognize the generation's common sensibilities while acknowledging that its members are unique individuals. Human resources has acknowledged that having unique experiences and attitudes is beneficial to the creativity and development of the organization. Now, organizations have an opportunity to learn from a vocal and innovative new workforce generation, the Zoomers.

In reality, individuals have always identified themselves in one group or another; they just didn't express it out loud as young people do today. For example, many people from prior generations have identified themselves by a specific religion, hobby, moral code, ethnic background, or other metric that shapes their thinking. The difference with Gen Z is that they are defining new associations and declining to be a part of some traditional associations, such as churches and clubs. And Gen Z are vocal about the associations they choose to embrace, while older generations are silent about their selections.

I'm not arguing that the world needs to be made aware of a person's sexual preferences, gender, religion, or any other personal characteristic. While Gen Z's outspoken voice swings the pendulum too far at times, many psychologists argue that it is mentally and physically healthier to communicate about what makes a person happy than to hold everything personal inside and never admit to inadequacies or struggles, or to having an affinity to a previously outcast group.

There is merit to questioning some of the stoicism of the past. When we look at conflicting opinions throughout history, it's clear that knowledge and communication have always been the key to understanding opposing per-spectives. Many people make assumptions about Gen Z based on a sound bite instead of taking time to understand the meaning behind its members' words. Sometimes, it's a simple matter of semantics and definitions, which we know have changed drastically over the generations.

EDUCATING MIXED MESSAGES OUT OF GEN Z

Gen Z, a generation that prides itself on living with purpose and strong values, sometimes makes purchasing, travel, and lifestyle choices that go against its stated beliefs. Zoomers advocate for social good and environmental steward-ship in business. However, their purchasing behavior often contradicts these values. For example, they take nearly as many international flights as domestic, they consume fast fashion, and they utilize power-heavy technology, without understanding the social, environmental, and financial impact of this and many other purchases.

One of the critical challenges for employers in understanding Gen Z is the generation's mixed messages. While the mixed messages of Gen Z pose a chal-lenge for employers, there is a potential for positive change. By teaching Gen Z how to make more informed decisions that are aligned with their purpose and values, leaders can significantly shift their decision-making and impact their approach to work and purchasing decisions. This potential for change should inspire hope and optimism in employers and business leaders.

As it relates to selecting and staying in a job, the opportunity to help Gen Z become knowledgeable about the truths of an organization lies with the employer. In the next section, I use fast fashion giant Shein as an example to illustrate Gen Z's conflicting messages and how education could change their behavior. My goal for this study is to show how Gen Z makes decisions without complete knowledge and how the same issue plagues employers when Gen Z is unclear about organizations' ethos and business practices. Educating Gen Z is not just a responsibility; it's also an opportunity for employers to shape these employees' behavior and loyalty to the organization by making them feel valued and integral to the company's operations.

Since Gen Z currently uses unreliable sources of information but is willing to learn and adopt new thinking about organizations, it follows that organiza-tions that take time during the recruiting process to educate them with facts about their business practices will earn higher candidate acceptance rates. As organizations offer transparency and proven progress toward continuously improving their practices, they will earn Gen Z's trust and loyalty. By understanding and aligning with Gen Z's values, employers can foster a stronger connection with their younger workforce. This potential for change should inspire and excite employers about the positive impact they can have on Gen Z's behavior and loyalty.

SHEIN'S STORY

Shein, a TikTok-famous retailer, distinguishes itself by focusing on rapid production cycles and an extensive inventory of fashion products priced at an average of $8 per item, constantly updated to reflect the latest consumer trends. The fast-growing fashion giant is a major contributor to waste, has questionable working conditions for its employees, and participates in unfair tax and tariff practices. Yet while Gen Z is known for its value sensibilities and focus on global health, it remains the largest consumer of Shein, and its members downloaded the merchandiser's app over three hundred million times in 2023.

To understand this better, I ran a focus group of Gen Z Shein consumers between the ages of eighteen and twenty-eight. I conducted interviews to measure how important ethics in business are to the participants' decision-making. All participants claimed that business ethics were "important" or "very important." They identified the top three ethics metrics as (1) impact on the environment, (2) employee welfare, and (3) business practices.

Then, without using the Shein brand name, I asked them for input on whether they would do business with an organization that conducted business as Shein does. For example, I explained the financial advantages that allow products to remain at the industry's lowest price point. The two examples I gave described the mock company's benefits gained from a Chinese law that waives tariffs on exports for direct-to-consumer (D2C) brands. Unlike traditional retailers that import and distribute merchandise in bulk, the company's products were individually packaged at the factory before being delivered to customers. This distribution approach allowed the company to take advantage of a long-standing US loophole that exempts packages worth up to $800 from import taxes if they are addressed and shipped to individuals.

Next, I approached the employee welfare concerns brought up by Gen Z. I explained to the participants that our mock company was mired in controversy for having violated labor laws, by forcing low-wage workers to complete seventy-five-hour shifts. I described the workers as working in workshops without safety protocols like windows and emergency exits.

Finally, I tackled participants' concerns about businesses' environmental impact. With over 80 percent of Gen Z reporting feeling anxious over global health, their willingness to overlook the negative environmental impact of fast fashion brands is confounding. I educated the participants on facts about fashion manufacturing. I explained that it is ranked third in global pollution causes and accounts for 10 percent of the annual carbon footprint: more than international flights and maritime shipping combined. I explained that according to the US Environmental Protection Agency, Americans discard approximately eighty-two pounds of textiles per person annually, most of which ends up in landfills[2]—and that most of our mock company's consumer-returned clothing went to a landfill due to the cost of refreshing, restocking, and reselling the same item again.

In all three areas of concern—honest business practices, environmental impact, and employee welfare—over 80 percent of the participants stated they would not do business with the organization described if they knew the truth about their business ethos. When I told my focus group the identity of the company I'd based my mock company on, 67 percent of the participants said they would no longer buy from Shein. The other 13 percent who hadn't changed their minds said they would "reconsider" or "buy less" but wouldn't commit to changing their buying behavior.

After that, I surveyed them on whether they would evaluate their employers on the same business ethos. They explained that what they considered important as consumers was also important to them as employees, as were diversity and employee benefits. When asked, 85 percent said they said they would immediately resign if they learned their employer used the same kind of business practices as the mock Shein company in my example. The other 15 percent said they would evaluate their response based on the specifics of what the company did.

I wanted to understand if they would change how they researched potential employers after learning about the mock Shein example. So I asked how they

---

2   Environmental Protection Agency (EPA), *Advancing Sustainable Materials Management: 2018 Fact Sheet,* December 2020, https://www.epa.gov/sites/default/files/2021-01/documents/2018_ff_fact_sheet_dec_2020_fnl_508.pdf.

had previously researched the essential measures of ethical business. Fifty-five percent acknowledged that before taking a job, they had conducted "no" or "very little" research and had simply accepted the role because it was "a foot in the door." This group also explained that because of what they'd learned from the mock Shein example, they felt they would do extensive, fact-based research when searching for their next job. The key takeaway is that they fully expected to leave the company, not stay loyal to their employer.

Those who did research before taking a job said they did so by using digital outlets such as social media and online job review sites; this method was followed by asking friends or family. While this approach is understandable, this reliance on personal networks and digital platforms raises concerns about the objectivity and reliability of the information Gen Z bases their decisions on. This group admitted they would do more extensive, fact-based research in the future, and not use subjective, opinion-based information exclusively.

Also interesting was the fact that 77 percent of all respondents claimed they used their intuition as a significant source for deciding on a role. In other words, they aren't using mainstream media investigatory insights, public financial reports, or reliable online news sources. Instead, they exclusively use opinion-based resources. This finding shows that as an employer, your effectiveness in inspiring the candidates and leaving them with a positive personal opinion about your organization is a highly important tool in bringing them on board.

This focus group summary indicates that it is important for organizations to educate young professionals on their business operations and ethos, particularly the issues that are important to Gen Z: impact on the environment, employee welfare, honest business practices, diversity, and benefits. Traditional recruiting focuses on role details and education or learned skills, whereas Gen Z professionals are interested in understanding your ethics profile.

PART TWO

EIGHT MYTHS ABOUT GEN Z

THEY'RE OVERCONFIDENT

Eighty-one percent of Gen Z thinks they can write a self-help book.

Yikes! That was my first thought when I read that statistic, which I discovered in a poll conducted by OnePoll and ThriftBooks. Then, as I tend to do, I thought there must be more to the story. I've worked with hundreds of members of Gen Z and I don't know many that would make such a claim without there being more to the story. So I conducted my own research to prove this wrong.

That plan backfired: It turns out this statement is true—sort of true, that is. But it is also very misleading, just as any single data point about an entire population is without context. Gen Z are not saying that they can write a self-help book today; what they are saying is that they have the tools and capabilities they would need to write a self-help book if they were tasked to or wanted to.

In my research, I show that Gen Z has confidence that they could write a self-help book for two key reasons. First, their entrepreneurial attitude has taught them that anything can be accomplished. Second, their formal education has taught them how to tackle big problems.

ENTREPRENEURIAL SPIRIT

Gen Z grew up in an entrepreneurial era. While Boomers and Gen X admired movie stars and rock stars, wallpapering their bedrooms with pages from celebrity magazines and throwing goodies on stage at concerts, Gen Z grew up admiring entrepreneurs. They respect and admire people who have built, improved, or invented products, services, and industries. They believe anything can be done with enough ingenuity and determination.

They have an entrepreneurial spirit, yet they also want to work for an organization that provides predictability and stability, positively impacting their mental well-being. Medium and large organizations offer more benefits, predictability, and stability. With all decisions, there is a trade-off that Gen Z has to resolve: entrepreneurial endeavors versus stability and predictability.

BIG PROBLEM-SOLVING

In their formal education, Gen Z have been taught to employ a combination of critical thinking and forensic thinking when solving big problems. They like to understand the overall mission and break it down into parts, solving each element of the overall project individually.

They've learned to tackle complex problems on teams and appreciate gathering multiple perspectives. With their technological savvy, they are able to aggregate information from multiple sources, analyze, and communicate their findings with confidence and clarity. Their recommendations will be understandable to a broad audience and will not include a lot of business jargon or filler words.

For Gen Z, writing a self-help book is simply another big problem to solve. They don't give the same weight to the traditional requirement of "having years of wisdom" before tackling a task. Right or wrong, the traits that they bring to an organization via their entrepreneurial and critical thinking are many of the same traits that leaders possess and that HR talent acquisition managers look for in contributor hiring.

PAT'S STORY

In 2019, I worked to collaboratively support the dairy industry: an industry that has a steadily declining share of consumer wallet, as well as low employee attraction and retention, and is experiencing an increasing disruptive trend toward nondairy "milk." The industry's promotion and innovation, which is funded by a 1983 government program called the Dairy Checkoff, was stuck in the previous century. With their mothers' encouragement, many Zoomers had stopped drinking milk, campaigned against megafarming, and become disinterested in working in the industry.

The organization responsible for the Dairy Checkoff went directly to the Zoomers for help. They recruited Pat and ten others to participate in a summer internship program to address the declining market growth and low engagement among their age group.

Pat, a twenty-year-old college junior, was offered the opportunity to lead the Zoomer interns. He was instructed to allocate an imaginary $10 million budget to drive market share and improve Gen Z's perception of the dairy industry. Pat and his team were given no other limitations.

Without intimidation or fear, the team created a collaboration that involved Gen Z's most popular video game and YouTube personality. Pat and his team presented their recommendations without hesitation or an ounce of doubt. The dairy industry ultimately executed the Gen Z program, and it became the single most-watched dairy promotion in history, with over three million views in twenty-four hours.

The tenacity, determination, and boldness of the young group of interns is reflective of their generation. They were fearless and unapologetic about jumping into a project for a $59 billion industry without hesitation. Their confident attitude is frequently misinterpreted as cockiness, hubris, or arrogance. Yet confidence is precisely the quality human resources and business leaders look for in employees. Gen Z is not afraid to jump in and solve problems; this is not a negative but a positive!

DEBUNKING THE MYTH

The myth about Gen Z is that they're overconfident. The truth is that they are fearless and confident that they can help solve big problems. Organizations that offer them challenging puzzles and allow flexibility in how they fix problems will discover that Gen Z's innovative, entrepreneurial spirit is a benefit to the organization, not a disruption.

Zoomers are confident that they can accomplish anything with enough hard work, creativity, and determination. They've learned to analyze with forensic, lateral, and creative thinking, in order to solve big problems. Few big problems appear overly daunting to them.

What Should You Do?

Given all that we've learned about Generation Z, you may be wondering how you can tap into their potential. Here are specific suggestions in nine areas that you can try.

USE THEIR ENTREPRENEURIAL SPIRIT

- Capture their creative and innovative thinking while training them on your company culture.

- Place them on cross-functional, cross-generational teams to allow them an opportunity to learn about different functions, roles, and business protocols from experienced contributors while sharing their fresh ideas.

- Foster autonomy by allowing them to reach the end goal using their methods, as long as their methods are preapproved and logical.

- Encourage them to take ownership by giving them full responsibility for projects, as well as the freedom to innovate and make decisions.

- Provide a flexible work environment by allowing them to choose where they sit in the office to maximize creativity and efficiency.

- Set challenging outcomes, not simple tasks.

- Explain the big picture and provide them with ambitious but achievable goals that lead to the desired outcome.

- Encourage opportunities for experimentation by allowing them free time to explore and discover new products, practices, approaches, and software, even if there's a risk of failure.

OFFER OPPORTUNITIES FOR LEARNING AND GROWTH

- Provide plenty of access to professional development courses, conferences, and mentorships that align with their interests.

- Allow them to explore areas outside their expertise to develop a broader skill set.

- Consider offering hobby or passion development opportunities that improve their emotional well-being and teach leadership skills—youth coaching or horseback riding lessons, for example.

RECOGNIZE AND REWARD INNOVATION AND EMBRACE A TOLERANCE FOR FAILURE

- Celebrate successes by acknowledging their contributions publicly and reward their innovative ideas. However, resist the "everyone gets a ribbon" approach to acknowledgment, which will reduce your credibility.

- Offer nonmonetary rewards like increased decision-making power, access to exclusive resources, or part-time management opportunities on a particular project.

- Normalize calculated risks that encourage creativity and frame failures as learning opportunities.

- Support resilience by offering guidance on overcoming setbacks and turning them into opportunities for growth.

ENCOURAGE NETWORKING AND COLLABORATION

- Facilitate connections by creating network resource groups to introduce them to other entrepreneurs, mentors, or thought leaders who can inspire and challenge them, knowing that together they help solve one another's problems.

- Encourage collaboration with diverse groups to stimulate creativity.

PROVIDE RESOURCES FOR CREATIVITY

- Equip them with reasonable access to tools and technology to help them bring ideas to life. (Nothing irritates young people more than antiquated technology and processes that aren't efficient!)

- Offer experimental individual R & D budgets for innovative ideas, projects, or initiatives.

SUPPORT THEIR VISION

- Understand what drives them and tailor opportunities to their aspirations.
- Actively listen to their ideas and provide constructive feedback.

ENABLE ENTREPRENEURIAL VENTURES

- Create intrapreneurship opportunities and allow young professionals to lead hypothetical initiatives within an organization—ones that could become budgeted programs within the organization.
- Encourage side projects that align with their entrepreneurial spirit.

CREATE A SENSE OF SHARED PURPOSE

- Connect your sub–mission statements with their values to foster intrinsic motivation. (Singular mission statements can have multiple sub–mission statements.)
- Show them impact metrics that point out the contributions they make to a tangible outcome.

EDUCATE THEM ON THE "HIDDEN INCOME" THEY RECEIVE BY WORKING FOR YOUR ORGANIZATION

- Calculate the monetary value of each benefit you offer and add it to their annual salary. For health insurance: Determine the annual employer contribution to premiums.
  For example:

  Employer pays $500/month for health insurance = $500 × 12 = $6,000/year.

- For retirement contributions: Calculate based on the employer match. For example:

  50 percent match on up to 6 percent of a $60,000 salary = $60,000 ×

6 percent × 50 percent = $1,800/year.

- For PTO: Calculate the value of paid time off by dividing the annual salary by the total workdays.
  For example:

  $60,000 salary/260 workdays = $230.77/day.

  If fifteen days of PTO are provided, the value is 15 × $230.77 = $3,461.55/year.

- For other benefits: Assign market values.
  For example:

  Gym membership = $50/month × 12 = $600/year.

  Tuition reimbursement = $5,000/year.

- For mentorship programs: Calculate the cost associated with taking another contributor away from their job to mentor the young professional.
  For example:

  $100,000 salary/2,080 work hours per year = $48.00/hour. An associate that spend one hour per month is a value of $575.00.

  This doesn't account for the opportunity loss or cost of taking the young professional out of their daily work.

THEY CAN'T COMMUNICATE

Several years ago, I was working with one of largest financial organizations in the country to build a young professional strategy. For this company, the work involved four parts: (1) understanding their young workforce, (2) training and coaching Gen Z, (3) training leaders and managers on how to effectively communicate and manage Gen Z contributors, and (4) cocreating sustainable programs to attract, recruit, onboard, and develop Gen Z.

First, using artificial intelligence, we were able to analyze and understand their specific young workforce in order to make informed decisions about human capital strategies and training programs. Relying on generalized information or assumptions about an entire generation is ineffective. Modern technology enables the collection and analysis of workforce data with precision, making it essential to base strategies and leadership training on insights specific to the organization's employees.

Second, Gen Z was trained and coached by implementing a Success Academy, a program that has a broad, encompassing curriculum that fills the gaps in their formal education. The company I was working with, and others like it, developed an academy of programs to guide practical business etiquette and professional behaviors that lead to career success for young professionals entering the workforce.

Third, robust HR initiatives were designed and built to enhance productivity, loyalty, and high performance across all generations while aligning with the organization's key performance indicators (KPIs).

I began as I always do: by assessing the current state of the company. I interviewed up, down, and sideways throughout the organization, gathering information and discovering what was working, what could be improved, and what could be removed from their current processes.

Eventually, I interviewed the chief economist of the organization, whose first question was "Why are they so sensitive?" She proceeded to tell me this story.

The organization had always recruited very high achievers, and this particular year was no exception. The company had their sights set on one graduate student, Trevor, who had already begun to make a name for himself in the industry. He had coauthored papers and researched alongside his academic mentors for several years, and he had earned respect from many leaders in the field of economics.

The company was successful in recruiting Trevor, and the chief economist decided that she would personally mentor him. At the end of his two-week onboarding, she invited Trevor to a client luncheon.

It was a typical business luncheon with big round tables and white tablecloths. The conversation was comfortable and casual as Trevor sat listening and observing, but also asking and answering questions as appropriate. The food was equally predictable, for the most part: salmon on a bed of greens and soda water with a lime. Then the server got to Trevor and delivered spaghetti with meatballs and a milkshake. The meal continued, and the meeting concluded with great promises of ongoing partnering and next steps.

On the way back to the office, the chief economist told Trevor that he shouldn't have ordered what he ordered because it "just doesn't look professional."

Trevor went to HR. He described the luncheon, explained that he worried he might lose his job, and asked for help.

Since the day the chief economist told me this story, I have repeated it to many leaders and other professionals throughout several organizations. I am always surprised by the strong emotion the story elicits from people in every generation. People take either one side of the debate or the other, with one side saying, "What does it matter what he orders? Can he do his job?" and the other side saying, "Why did he go to HR? Why didn't he just go to his manager or even talk about it more with the chief economist?"

I knew there must be more to the story, so I interviewed Trevor. I learned that he had been raised humbly in a small, rural American town by a hardworking father and mother: a factory worker and a restaurant server. He had devoted his high school and college years to academics.

He had never been to a formal, high-level business lunch before the one with the chief economist. When he was handed a menu full of foods prepared in ways he was unfamiliar with, he chose the only meal that he felt confident ordering. It was a family favorite. And, after all, *it was on the menu.*

The lunch was the first time he had met the chief economist. At the time of the invitation Trevor didn't know that she planned on mentoring him. He thought every new associate at the organization got to lunch with an executive as part of their onboarding. Likewise, since he had been in onboarding for two weeks and had only met his hiring manager during the interview process, he didn't feel he knew them well enough to ask for help, and he didn't want to "seem needy." Yet he wanted "someone's advice."

When the chief economist told him he shouldn't have ordered spaghetti, he felt worried about his job. In his mind, he had been reprimanded by one of the highest-ranking officers of the organization, and the damage was career threatening.

During onboarding, the HR representative had frequently counseled that everyone should feel comfortable going to HR for help if they had any concerns or questions. Trevor had gone to the person at the organization he felt he knew the best: the HR facilitator of his onboarding. He said that he'd sought advice and help to get on "good terms again" with the chief economist.

The situation eventually worked out, and they are now both mentoring each other. However, the issue may have been prevented with better understanding and communication. The chief economist could have been clear about her expectations and her intentions to mentor Trevor. And Trevor could have asked her for the rationale behind her comment. Instead, the chief economist made a generalization and assumption, telling me that "Gen Z is weird" and "too sensitive."

As cultures, traditions, protocols, and behaviors in the workforce are increasingly becoming more diverse, leaders who expect historical uniformity will create misunderstandings and cause their young professionals to demonstrate unexpected behaviors.

The beauty of this and many other stories with similar outcomes is that many problems may be averted with strong communication. While there are differences in the ways people communicate, there is always a reason for their thoughts, ideas, and behaviors. Being willing to take the time to explore a person's rationale before making assumptions about them is the single most important way to build strong teams.

THE SPAGHETTI GENERATION

Common complaints I hear about Gen Z revolve around what people describe as their inability to fit in and act appropriately in business environments; I hear statements like "They act weird," "They don't look a person in the eyes," "They dress like slobs or hookers," "They don't know how to communicate," "They have no social skills," and "They're clueless on how to behave."

These and many more labels that plague Gen Z can be resolved with understanding, communication, and empathy.

> As the most diverse generation in US history, Gen Z will bring new habits, lingo, and preferences to their communication style.

Human Versus Business Communication

What's become increasingly apparent in business is that communication is separated into two types: business communication and human communication. The higher you go up the corporate ladder, the more business communication is used and the less human communication is used. It makes sense that as you have more responsibility in the organization and attend more meetings, you use more business communication and less common, conversational language.

While both are important, business communication teaches about business. It informs younger professionals about what to look for in strategies, how to resolve conflicts, how to negotiate with grace, how to ask difficult questions, how to extract important financial details from a business, and a host of other important business skills.

Human communication, on the other hand, builds trust and confidence. People who feel they can approach a leader regardless of their seniority, and who speak in their honest voice, gain confidence. Trust and confidence breed improved performance.

As organizations flatten and become more collaborative, the combining of business and human communications will become increasingly important to the success of the organization. Cross-generational, cross-functional collaborative teams will inevitably be built, to the benefit of the organization. Unique and wide-ranging thoughts and perspectives create a way to brainstorm fresh ideas.

They Don't Know How to Communicate

One bias against Gen Z that runs deep throughout the mature generations is expressed by the idea that "they don't know how to communicate," which is a statement I hear nearly daily from members of older generations. Yes, they do. They simply do it differently than older people. Each generation idealizes their way of behaving and communicating, offering little appreciation and grace for the way different generations behave and communicate.

Remember, the Gen Z worker got a job at your organization, so they must have communicated well enough for that!

ADAPTING TO GEN Z

Every generation has adapted to the tools and challenges of their time, and Gen Z is no exception. Growing up in a world defined by rapid technological advancements, they've developed an approach to communication that emphasizes speed, efficiency, and purpose. Older generations may initially find their reliance on text messages or digital platforms impersonal, but it's worth looking deeper.

Gen Z's preference for quick, tech-forward interactions isn't a rejection of connection; it's an evolution. For simple tasks, they prioritize convenience, reserving live communication for meaningful, complex conversations. This approach is not about avoiding human interaction but about optimizing it for what truly matters. Their methods reflect adaptability, resourcefulness, and a respect for time—qualities that are valuable to performance and productivity in any era.

Gen Z, known for their digital fluency, often gravitate toward quick, efficient, and tech-forward communication methods, especially for tasks or issues that don't require extensive discussion. From their perspective, texts, emails, and messaging apps are ideal for resolving straightforward matters, seeking simple instructions, or getting quick support. This preference reflects their desire to save time and streamline interactions in a fast-paced world. Picking up a phone, dialing, and waiting for an answer is simply wasted time in the minds of Gen Z. To them, a call causes an interruption of thought and activity; sending a text or email is more thoughtful to others and efficient for everyone.

However, many people overlook that Gen Z also values live and face-to-face communication when there is a purpose for it. Zoomers believe live conversations should be reserved for deep, meaningful, or complex discussions that require emotional nuance, brainstorming, or collaborative problem-solving. In their view, these moments of live interaction foster stronger connections and lead to better outcomes when the stakes are higher or the context is more intricate.

This duality underscores Gen Z's pragmatic approach to communication: leveraging technology for simple matters while preserving personal interaction for situations that truly benefit from it. Understanding this balance can improve how a company supports and respects its tech-savvy and deeply practical communication generation.

For older generations, this shift presents a unique opportunity. Rather than viewing Gen Z's communication style as a threat to traditional protocol, they can be embrace it as a chance to learn and grow. Understanding how to navigate and embrace technology advancements is essential for staying connected in an increasingly digital world. By engaging with Gen Z using their chosen methods, older generations can foster stronger relationships across the age gap and enhance their tech literacy and communication efficiency.

The key is mutual respect. Gen Z can learn from older generations' interpersonal depth and experience, while older generations can gain insight into the innovative ways Gen Z leverages technology to communicate. By embracing these differences, we can bridge generational divides and create a richer, more connected future for everyone.

LORETTA'S STORY

Loretta runs an insurance agency. The old-school way, with manila folders that hold vast amounts of important data and information. The kind of crucial information that would be used in court if a claim were disputed.

Loretta uses the desk phone to make and take calls. For ninety-one years the family has been running the business over the phone. These days, business is slowing down. Loretta is finding it difficult to bring in new young contributors and clients. She says that she is "frustrated and confused by these young people."

Without doubt, Gen Z wants to work for a company that utilizes modern technology to make their jobs efficient, logical, and simple. They also will only trust their purchases to a company they perceive as modern and secure. They want to know that their information and data are stored securely, using technology, not paper files. And they prefer having quick customer service conversations by chat, text, or email—not a phone call.

Modernize your business and communications to attract Gen Z as contributors and as customers.

FORMALIZE CROSS-GENERATIONAL TEAMS

Subjectivity dominates all relationships. Individual perspectives, feelings, and opinions largely influence relationships. In other words, a person's experiences and interpretations of relationships can vary widely. And though the measurement of trust is personal to each individual, there are universal ways to achieve trust.

Companies achieve trust through open and honest communication, consistent follow-through on commitments, and a culture of transparency. Gen Z contributors are loyal when they trust that their managers focus on their well-being, not just profitability. The best way to achieve mutual loyalty is through communication and collaboration.

There's no one-size-fits-all approach or objective measure for understanding or managing cross-generational relationships, as individual perceptions and emotions shape them. Yet one thing is generally true: Building solid relationships requires communication, mutual respect, trust, and understanding. For instance, active listening, regular feedback, and empathy are key tools in managing professional relationships.

According to psychologist Robert Plutchik's theory of emotion, humans can experience over thirty-four thousand unique emotions. Now, add to that the range of intensity each emotion carries and there is an infinite array of emotions that influence behavior. To build a relationship, people need to navigate this emotional cacophony by communicating effectively and trying to understand one another.

Many great leaders hire for skill sets they don't possess, often in industries outside of their own. Successful leaders and organizations hope for new, fresh ideas. Often, bringing in unique perspectives and accepting new ways of thinking delivers inspiring ideas that would otherwise be missed. In deeply collaborative work environments, contributors learn from managers and managers learn from contributors, fostering a culture of continuous learning and inspiration.

Organizations that rely on creativity often embrace diverse thinking, but many other functions effectively silo project teams and neglect to include all generations and functions. Yet mutual respect occurs when mature contributors see firsthand what fresh ideas Gen Z brings. Gen Z contributors in turn learn from the experience of the mature generations, fostering a culture of mutual respect.

Trust builds when contributors throughout the organization construct relationships with one another.

KERRY'S STORY

An engraved wooden frame housing a photo of Kerry in his US Air Force uniform was positioned next to the crystal trophy engraved with his name, given as thanks for his service at his company as an airplane engineer. Both were proudly displayed in Kerry's home office, surrounded by a hoard of airplane memorabilia. You see, Kerry was one of the few people who'd defined his dream job at age five and never changed his mind. He had manifested his dream life.

His civilian job hadn't been easy to secure, even though he had stellar commendations from the Air Force. "It's not easy getting a role at the most respected air engineering organization in the world," he explained. So when he earned the spot, he'd moved his family and begun life as a cherished, respected contributor.

Over the following years, he was always motivated and enthused to share his practical expertise regarding materials and structure, as well as his flight experience, to research, develop, and improve his company's airplanes. He was honored to tell people, even strangers, how he contributed to the aircraft manufacturing industry, worth half a trillion dollars.

The company leadership regularly sought and took his input and advice on new concepts. Until they didn't. New leadership in the company continued to solicit input and guidance, but they stopped taking the valuable, talented, experienced engineers' advice. It wasn't just Kerry they began to ignore, it was his whole team. And many other teams as well—teams that also had expertise, experience, and warnings to issue to leadership.

Kerry said that at first, he thought it was an oversight. Soon, he began to ask others at the organization if they were experiencing the same thing. People continued to raise red flags about the new aircraft in several areas of concern, but the development and manufacturing schedule didn't change.

Concern turned into panic, panic turned into disgust, and disgust turned into Kerry's resignation. Kerry could not work for a company that he recognized was putting company profits above respect for its engineers, its workforce, the local community economy, its business partners, its customers, its end users, and its reputation.

You may recognize this company as Boeing, the US company that carried such American pride that citizens proudly wore lapel pins with the tagline "If it's not Boeing, I'm not going." Today, accidents due to safety issues with their products have cost the company four billion US dollars and an incalculable amount in human loss and suffering. Kerry and his colleagues continue to mourn the loss of the employees who took their lives as a result.

In Kerry's words, "The company cares more about profitability than safety or anything else." Boeing is an extreme example of leadership working in a vacuum and disrespecting its associates by not listening and heeding their advice. In some public disclosures, and according to Kerry's insider's perspective, Boeing leadership mocked their associates and made it clear through their incentive programs that many unrealistic production timelines were not negotiable, despite the raising of safety concerns.

Boeing hasn't officially disclosed the number of associates it has lost, but Kerry claims there are hundreds of contributors who left or plan to leave. He says others cannot leave because of retirement timelines, but have essentially quiet quit, no longer motivated or inspired to give Boeing their all.

Essentially, Boeing violated several important tenets of the employer-employee relationship:

- Mutual respect was broken when the company disregarded the input of its contributors.
- Trust was shattered when the organization prioritized profitability above everything else.
- Communication was flawed throughout the entire end-to-end project.

IMMEDIATE IMPACT

An organization can build cross-generational relationships by increasing warm social support systems like mentoring, advice, and collaboration and by decreasing strain and cold systems like apathy, criticism, and demand making. Strong cross-functional and cross-generational connections give contributors a valuable sense of meaning and purpose, improve communication skills, and benefit overall well-being.

While most young professionals don't have experience building relationships in a multigenerational environment, the young people I have counseled in my work all admit that their lives would be better if they had stronger mentors and social connections. Secondary and postgraduate schools and many organizations continue to offer ways for young people to find comfort by participating in clubs, activities, and events to find their like-minded people. However, members of Gen Z have yet to learn how to be comfortable when they are not among like-minded individuals.

Up until this time, Gen Z has chosen the teams they belong to based on their personal interests: football, band, robotics, sorority, and so on. Their first professional role often put them in the position, for the first time, of having no choice in who they were teamed with. Contributors tell me that one of the greatest outcomes of their company's talent development and relationship-building efforts is their relationships with people from varied backgrounds, who have a range of outlooks on a variety of topics.

The younger generations have embraced the concept of "chosen family," which works in the organization's favor. It means that they are able and willing to find nurturing, mutually beneficial relationships outside of their traditional ones. In other words, workforce relationships can become influential, integral, and accepted relationships that Gen Z cherishes.

A character trait that's evident in most Zoomers I work with is a willingness to present and discuss ideas that older generations would have found uncomfortable. Here again, mutual respect plays a role. Generation Z won't blindly accept what they're told; they will ask for more information. They thrive on learning the rationale behind what they're told. They will engage in discussions and collaborate, even with those they don't have a historical relationship with, if it helps them understand the topic better.

Gen Z will listen to people regardless of age, background, or any other demographic and will share their own opinions. In turn, they want to be heard, and they expect counterarguments to their input to be logical. Gen Z will only bow to traditional ways that are cemented in logic; they will challenge traditions and work hard to improve ones that need to be revised. Gen Z members are curious and want to learn, but their loyalty hinges upon consistent and accurate information.

This mutual respect and collaboration will work in your organization's favor. You will gather inspiring, creative ideas and discover innovative processes by which to achieve goals. If they lack respect for their management or organization, however, Gen Z will either quiet quit, as many of Kerry's colleagues did, seek new employment, or do things their way, causing new issues for the organization that relies upon systems and processes.

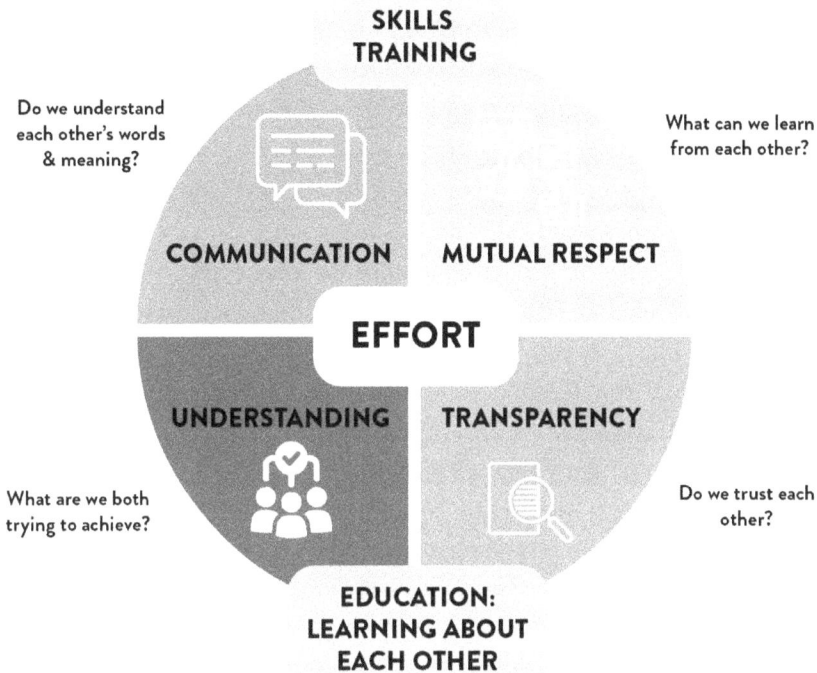

SKILLS TRAINING

Do we understand each other's words & meaning?

What can we learn from each other?

COMMUNICATION   **MUTUAL RESPECT**

EFFORT

UNDERSTANDING   **TRANSPARENCY**

What are we both trying to achieve?

Do we trust each other?

EDUCATION: LEARNING ABOUT EACH OTHER

DEBUNKING THE MYTH

The myth about Gen Z is that they can't communicate, won't pick up a phone, and don't type in complete sentences. Those statements are partly true—and all of those behaviors can create efficiencies in a workplace. Gen Z uses the best communication tools to accomplish their goals. They may appear like they aren't working as hard because they prefer to use efficient tools that are appropriate for each situation.

Leaders tell me their young professionals cannot assimilate and fit into workplace cultures. Older generations mistakenly think that because young professionals are highly educated, they understand the subtext behind their colleagues' and leaders' behaviors. Remember that young professionals frequently have formal education, but many don't have mentors and parents who taught them business protocol, and very few learned practical business lessons in school.

What Should You Do?

Educate your young professionals on the behavior you expect in your workforce. Present your business protocol as a path of personal development that will further their long-term business success. Gen Z will embrace what they learn.

I've emphasized the importance of building relationships within the organization, but another type of networking is equally crucial: external networking. Together, these two forms of networking teach the most impactful communication skills a person should have.

Networking, whether done within or outside the organization, is the key tool for building relationships. Note that networking is not just a business skill, but also a life skill. Teaching contributors to network will help them to find doctors, plan vacations, forge friendships, kindle romances, pursue new roles, secure new hires, and explore many other subjects.

Most importantly, your Zoomers will learn how to build and nurture their professional networks. Organizations benefit from teaching their contributors how to network, and the networks of your contributors are, by extension, your organization's network.

Teach Your Contributors to Network

If you teach your contributors to network correctly, you will reap benefits.

Your organization's network is an extension of your contributors' network. Here are some keys to help them build theirs:

- Key Number One: Teach them to do it before they think there's a need. If they build a network throughout their careers, it will be there when they need it.

- Key Number Two: Teach them to learn to enjoy the networking process. Remind them that they will boost their own emotional well-being when they do small, positive networking tasks, like wishing someone well on a job promotion or remembering someone's birthday.

- Key Number Three: Teach them to be rigorous and consistent in their networking. Help them learn the importance of using a software customer relationship management tool, a personal relationship management software tool, or a spreadsheet to manage their personal network. Now let's look at each of these in more detail.

KEY NUMBER ONE: BUILD IT BEFORE YOU NEED IT!

"Dialing for dollars" describes the practice of making numerous telephone calls to solicit business, donations, or sales. The phrase originated from a television show format in which hosts would call viewers randomly and offer them a chance to win money if they could answer a question correctly. In a business context, the phrase typically refers to salespeople or telemarketers making cold calls to potential customers to generate sales or leads. The goal is to reach as many people as possible to maximize potential revenue.

Unfortunately, we now have a social media platform that enables networking for dollars. I say unfortunately because I've fallen victim countless times to people who send a LinkedIn request to connect—almost before my finger lifts from the accept button, I receive their follow-up message about how they can fix my business problem. To date, 100 percent of the people who have reached out to me in this manner have had zero to offer me. None of them understood my business, much less what my business issues are.

This aggressive and random outreach method is not only ineffective but also off-putting. Those people may be a connection, but they are not a genuine part of my network. A better way to connect is the old-fashioned way: building a relationship over time. Then when you need to ask for advice, input, or business, your network will be receptive.

While sales teams' profitability may hinge on aggressive tactics, for most business professionals, a more patient, long-term approach to networking is the key to success. Networking is a lifelong, rewarding practice. By teaching your team the art of networking, you're benefiting not just them individually but also the organization as a whole.

KEY NUMBER TWO: LEARN TO ENJOY THE NETWORKING PROCESS

Here's simple yet powerful advice: Teach contributors to enjoy the networking process. When they start to see networking as an opportunity to connect, learn, and grow and meet new friends, rather than as a chore, they'll find it much more rewarding. When your contributors learn to view networking as supporting other human beings and making others feel good, the urgency and networking-for-dollars aspect are removed from the process.

We all know people who love giving gifts more than receiving them or volunteer their time because it makes them feel good. Networking is the business equivalent of those feel-good activities.

KEY NUMBER THREE: BECOME RIGOROUS AND CONSISTENT IN NETWORKING

People are busy. Your contributors must learn to stay dedicated and consistent in their networking. Organizations that provide networking training and give their contributors time in the month for networking will see the benefits manifested throughout their workforce. It takes little time. A thirty-minute Lunch and Learn session, followed by ongoing monthly networking time, will create the contributor networks you and your teams can be proud of.

Your organization's network is an extension of your contributors' network. Helping them build their networks will build yours as well.

THEY DON'T KNOW HOW TO WORK HARD

Members of Gen Z do exceptionally well when they are assigned outcomes, not tasks. They are motivated when they can participate in meaningful outcomes.

Gallup's State of the Global Workplace, a sobering viewpoint of the cost of employee disengagement, "estimates that low engagement costs the global economy $8.8 trillion. That's 9 percent of global GDP—enough to make the difference between success and a failure for humanity."[3] This is a call for immediate action, not just for the sake of the workforce but for the survival of our global economy.

According to a 2024 survey by chief executives, 60 percent of CEOs consider retaining and engaging employees their top priority in 2025, up from 57 percent in 2022. Second in CEO importance: improving cost structure. My friend Sally would have enjoyed her last eleven years at work if she'd been engaged in meaningful work that boosted her emotional well-being. Instead of what many organizations termed a "high-potential associate," she was viewed as a person at the end of her career, and resources were not spent on personal development plans for people in her situation. Instead, they were left to wither, and they became severely burned out and anxious to retire to find happiness.

Focusing on mutual engagement across generations and activating all workforce populations holds the promise of improving profitability and enhancing an organization, painting a hopeful picture of the future. Under cross-generational, collaborative conditions, generations understand they have valuable life experiences that can be used to mentor and guide one another. Gen Z, if asked, will gladly educate mature generations on their mindset, their buying

---

3   Gallup, "State of the Global Workplace," 2024, https://www.gallup.com/workplace/349484/state-of-the-global-workplace.aspx.

behavior, their values, and what motivates and engages them. Knowing all of that will make your HR program development easier.

WHY PEOPLE DISENGAGE

Gallup's latest State of the Global Workplace Report 2024 indicates that 21 percent of employees globally are engaged.[4] That leaves 79 percent disengaged. Disengagement isn't new, but it's shocking how prevalent it is and that it continues to pick up momentum. People disengage at work, as they do during other activities, when they aren't inspired by, consumed with, or enjoying what they're doing. Gen Z, like all people, want to be engaged at work. They want to know that their work is valued and respected and has a direct and vital impact on the company's success. Every person in the organization contributes to its success, but sadly, many are never told that they are appreciated for their contributions. In a siloed or large organization, it is difficult for most people to see the connection between their role and the overall success of the organization.

Roughly eighty million people, or 39 percent of working Americans, report having a side hustle. The majority are hustling for more money, to acquire new skills, or for passion. And, if they were able, 65 percent of side hustlers say they'd prefer having one source of income rather than many.[5]

These side hustlers believe they have more potential than they are using in their paid positions. They feel they could capitalize on their unrealized potential and succeed in their own businesses.

Despite the prevailing opinion that this Gen Z ideology is new, it is not. People have wanted to achieve their greatest potential for generations. Many associates have long felt they were not given an opportunity to reach their highest potential and were held back by bureaucratic or discriminatory corporate politics and policies. Many believed they could achieve greater happiness if they worked for themselves.

Edward Higgins studied this attitude in 1987 and incorporated it into his self-discrepancy theory. The theory discusses the gaps between the actual self, the ideal self, and the self one ought to be able to attain based on that person's

---

4   Gallup, "State of the Global Workplace."

5   Lane Gillespie, "Survey: 39% Have a Side Hustle, and 44% Believe They'll Always Need One," *Bankrate*, May 24, 2023, https://www.bankrate.com/personal-finance/side-hustle-survey. Matt Schulz, "2025 Side Hustle Survey: Nearly 2 in 5 Americans Have a Side Hustle, With 3 in 5 Saying the Income Is Essential," LendingTree, accessed May 30, 2025, https://www.lendingtree.com/debt-consolidation/side-hustle-income-survey/.

own interpretation of themselves. Today, Gen Z leads the charge in arguing that an ideal self and the self they should be able to attain are the same. They believe the ideal self is attained by having a life–work balance.

In essence, Gen Z want a defined measure of success and some flexibility in how to achieve that success. They want to take ownership in achieving their highest potential. This desire to have ownership is what causes some people to leave organizations and make their side hustles their full-time careers. They believe they can reach their potential without the organization and be happier in life doing so.

The self-discrepancy gap, the gap between actual and ideal self, decreases when a contributor experiences holistic well-being. By experiencing their highest emotional, mental, and physical well-being, they expect to contribute to society at their highest potential.

In the workplace, when the gap is too vast, Zoomers feel they have three primary options for resolution. They can discuss the issue with their manager, leadership, or talent development representative and work through career path revisions. They can quiet quit, which is the term for continuing to be physically present at work but disengaging by putting little incremental or creative effort into their roles. These contributors are often seeking new employment or participating in a side hustle that brings them joy. Or, they can leave the organization.

For most contributors, the three options are considered in order: First, speak to a company representative. Next, disengage or quiet quit, and finally, when nothing changes, resign from the role. Again, Gen Z is different; they may not take long to progress through the three options. As I mentioned previously, as soon as they feel disenchanted or duped, they resign.

THE COST OF DISENGAGED GEN Z CONTRIBUTORS

Regardless of whether everyone agrees with Gen Z's mentality, we need them in our workforce. Their progressive thinking is forcing organizations to take notice, adapt, and innovate, prompting changes within human resource departments and talent management. Remember that Generation Z is most animated on the topic, and they are teaching the mature generations to rethink their own life–work balance.

The following table shows the average costs of losing members of Gen Z. The numbers are based on data reported by reputable organizations within the HR industry. Consider these statistics and the costs associated with losing Gen Z:

- For entry-level roles up through mid-level positions, the time to find a job averages eight weeks.

- SHRM reports that on average for all levels of contributors, it costs a company six to nine months of an employee's salary to replace. Not all Gen Z members are employed at an entry level; for that reason, the last column of the table reflects a six-month period to replace them, using the same entry-level salary.

- Twenty-seven percent of the workforce will be Gen Z by 2025.

- HR leaders predict that 44 percent of Gen Z employees will likely quit within the next six months due to a lack of support for their career development.

COSTS OF REPLACING GEN Z WHEN THEY LEAVE AN ORGANIZATION

Size of company based on number of contributors	Number of Gen Z contributors: 27% of workforce in 2025	Number of Gen Z contributors who will leave w/in 6 months: 44%	Cost of replacing 44% of Gen Z: two-months' salary scenario	Cost of replacing 44% of Gen Z: six-months' salary scenario
500	135	60	$494,920	$1,484,762
1,000	270	119	$989,841	$2,969,524
5,000	1,350	594	$4,949,208	$14,847,624
10,000	2,700	1,188	$9,898,416	$29,695,248
20,000	5,400	2,376	$19,796,832	$59,390,496
50,000	13,500	5,940	$49,492,080	$148,476,240
100,000	27,000	11,880	$98,984,160	$296,952,480

The numbers are staggering. Use the calculations in this chart to determine your own risk of ignoring Gen Z as an essential contributor in your organization.

Keep in mind that this is a snapshot calculation, meaning that the calculations fluctuate throughout the year based on your hiring seasonality. In many organizations, January through May shows an increase in entry-level hires, which skews the annual numbers. This calculation is increasingly accurate when calculated over a year.

The annual cost to retain the Gen Z contributors who leave your organization is equal to the amount you should budget for a long-term retention program. A robust retention program will offset the cost of the recruiting and retaining process. More importantly, it will eliminate the unseen costs associated with losing contributors. These include:

- The cost of low morale and of unmotivated contributors who have to pick up the slack when their teammates leave.

- The cost of high turnover as a sign of instability.

- The cost of missed deadlines and project timelines due to the adjustment period of bringing new associates up to speed.

- The cost of key initiatives that might be delayed or abandoned due to resource shifts.

- The cost of high turnover to the company's reputation among prospective hires, making it harder to attract top talent.

- The cost of negative public perception due to exiting contributors publicly voicing their negative experience.

- The cost of departing employees taking creative ideas or strategies with them, especially if they join competitors.

HOW TO CALCULATE COSTS OF LOW RETENTION

Example	Your Company's Numbers
Number of Gen Z contributors in your organization.	100
Number of Gen Z contributors that leave in the first year.	20
Your company's entry-level salary.	$40,000
Monthly salary = annual salary/12	$3,333/ month
Number of months it takes your company to fill an empty role.	3
Cost per contributor to fill their role.	$3,333 x 3 months = $9,999
Annual cost to fill all Gen Z roles when they leave your organization.	$199,980

Sixty-one percent of disengaged associates are actively seeking new roles.

"I don't feel like I'm making a difference at work. I feel bored and it's going to take ten years to be in a job that I like." —C. Y., Gen Z individual contributor

> **"I've been promoted and gotten a raise, but I still don't feel like this is the best role for me."**
> **—P. D., Gen Z individual contributor**

The biggest misperception about Gen Z is that they are demanding.

DEBUNKING THE MYTH

The myth about Gen Z is that they don't want to or know how to work hard. That is simply not true. Gen Z is motivated when assigned meaningful outcomes, not tasks. They need to understand that their role has an essential contribution to the organization's overall success.

More than any prior generation, Gen Z is looking for a contribution and meaning in their careers. They are not lazy—they have accomplished a lot in their young lives. But they must be motivated. If they aren't motivated and feeling aligned with their employer, they will leave quickly, within six months.

What Should You Do?

Since Gen Z is outcome driven and wants to understand that their contribution is meaningful, it's best to show the connection between their roles and the larger picture of the organization and the world.

Few organizations educate their employees on the entire scope of their business operations. The majority prioritize training specific-to-individual roles, while only a fraction offer comprehensive cross-functional training programs that encompass the entire business process.

Many employees, not just Gen Z, lack an understanding of how other departments within their organization interconnect to drive overall success. They often don't realize how decisions in one department can create ripple effects throughout the business, impacting finance, operations, and strategic goals. This lack of awareness can lead to misaligned priorities, inefficiencies, and missed opportunities for collaboration.

For example, employees in sales may not understand the constraints faced by supply chain or production teams. This failure to consider operational limitations can lead to poor customer service and communications. Similarly, marketing teams might propose campaigns without fully grasping the campaigns' financial implications on operations. Without a holistic view of the business, employees are more likely to work in silos, creating disconnects that hinder organizational performance.

Formal training programs rarely address this issue, focusing instead on role-specific skills without connecting the dots between departments. This creates a workforce that is technically proficient but lacks the broader business understanding needed to make informed decisions. Employees often fail to see how their individual roles contribute to the company's larger goals, which leads to their feeling disengagement and a sense of being undervalued.

Organizations can address this gap by implementing the following:

- Cross-functional training programs that expose employees to the operations of other departments.

- Job shadowing, rotational assignments, and cross-departmental projects that provide hands-on learning.

- Workshops and internal seminars led by team leaders to shed light on how various functions work together to achieve the company's objectives.

- Education of associates on the key performance indicators of their colleagues to illustrate why they make decisions that appear to be counterintuitive to another associate.

By prioritizing end-to-end business education, organizations can foster a culture of collaboration and shared accountability. Employees who understand the bigger picture are more engaged, motivated, and equipped to contribute meaningfully to their company's success.

THEY ALL WANT TO HAVE A DREAM JOB AND WORK FROM HOME

My research shows that 75 percent of Generation Z members want variety, not a five-days-per-week work-from-home job. They want the flexibility that allows them to benefit from the camaraderie and development that occur by working in the office a couple of days a week. They also see a benefit in saving time and money by skipping the commute, eating at home, and dressing comfortably at a remote office for a portion of the workweek. And they are very clear that they must produce quality work regardless of where they sit to work.

Remote management is not new. Founders, CEOs, and leaders from most industries have long had teams that reside and work in another plant, building, town, state, or country. For some reason, Gen Z has been credited with inventing a new remote work philosophy, though this approach has been around for decades.

The difference today is that remote work is now also offered in the same town as a company's office; historically, remote work existed to expand the business's reach or because inexpensive land mandated where new facilities could be built. The accompanying workforce was a remote one in order to fill distant distribution centers and satellite sales offices, to consult where customers' offices were located, and to meet needs created by many other workplace scenarios.

Today, remote work means variety. Young professionals want to have an ability to choose to work occasionally from a local café, home office, airport, or other location. Leaders who accommodate flexibility while setting clear and firm expectations and KPIs for their remote workers will see improved performance, not the opposite.

The Gen Z request is to find a balanced life with variety and one that supports their life–work balance, not a request to work less.

THEY WANT A DREAMY JOB

Older generations have snidely rebuked Gen Z for asking for such a lofty career prize as a dream job and life–work balance. However, recently, the student has become the teacher concerning career and life. Gen Z have created a movement toward searching for their optimum role, but it is quickly spreading to other generations. Contributors across all generations, functions, and businesses are asking their employers to support their success by helping them align their career, lifestyle, family, and personal growth—all while impacting the world.

Gen Z are seeking purpose in life and career. They believe that work should have a purpose, not just be a job.

Many people roll their eyes at Gen Z's audacity in wanting a perfect career, but it has been indoctrinated into them by older generations. In some cases, they have been misdirected about career and work throughout their lives. Many have been instructed—by everyone from pop culture icons to coaches, educators, parents, and countless speakers giving well-intended commencement speeches—to "dream big" and "shoot for the stars."

PEOPLE LIKE TO DO WHAT THEY'RE GOOD AT: FINDING A DREAM JOB

I have worked with young adults throughout my life, helping them identify, decipher, and work to achieve their life's aspirations. The single most common question I get when I speak to young professionals or college students is "How do I find my dream job?"

The term *dream job* is loosely defined and means something different to everyone. People have been talking about dream jobs for decades. It made me wonder: How is dream job defined? Do many people have dream jobs? How do they know if they have a dream job, and how did they find it?

I began to conduct research to understand more about dream jobs and how to help people find them. It turns out that while people have been in search of dream jobs for decades, fewer than one out of ten people claim to actually have one.

DREAMY JOB = SKILLS + ATTRIBUTES + FUTURE VISION

This equation seems simple, but it has deep emotional and psychological elements that help to define a career direction. Let's unravel the equation.

Skills

These are the precise, teachable capabilities that are measurable and often job specific. They include learned techniques like accounting, software programming, communication, and problem-solving.

Attributes

Many companies post open roles that have a heavy focus on skills, but in addition to skills, a high-quality hire should embody the attributes required for the role. These hidden personality traits inform a person's thoughts and behaviors. For example, an introvert may prefer the quiet and solitude of an enclosed office, while an extrovert may prefer an open workplace or no office at all.

> Some attributes are formed by genetics or upbringing. Many can be shaped over time with effort and guidance.

Hiring can easily go off track when a talent acquisition team focuses solely on skills without considering attributes. Consider training, for example. For all functions and experience levels, many job postings use the word *training*.

The issue with broadly defining jobs using a term like *training* is that a training role can require vastly different attributes. For instance, a detail-oriented and empathetic individual might excel in a training role that allows them to design training materials because they intuitively understand what a learner needs to know in order to feel capable. Yet that same person might feel uncomfortable leading training sessions or presenting in front of an audience. On the other hand, an engaging trainer who loves being in front of an audience may struggle to put fingertips on the keyboard to write the content. This is an example of two vastly different personality types with different attributes filling a role with the same requirement: training. Asking the same person to do both the writing and training may result in mediocre performance of both the creation and the presenting.

This highlights an important truth: Hiring for any role requires understanding not just the skills needed but also the personality traits that align with the specific demands of the position. In the training example above, whether the role involves public speaking, one-on-one coaching, or behind-the-scenes content development, the right candidate must possess the unique combination of skills and attributes that fit the role's requirements.

Talent acquisition teams can avoid mismatches and build a stronger, more effective workforce by taking a more nuanced approach to job postings and candidate evaluation.

Future Vision

Being skilled and having aligned attributes can lead to having a dream job, but there must also be a future vision. *Future vision* is the intensely personal concept of how someone sees their personal and professional life blending seamlessly in the future. It is the picture a person has in their head of how they want to live. For example, does the person see themselves in a bustling city with a C-suite role, in a job they can leave at the end of the day to go fishing, be with children, or visit nearby family? There is no limit to the options. Future vision includes anything that creates a perfect lifestyle people envision for themselves.

While most successful people acknowledge the importance of setting goals, few take the time to craft a clear and inspiring picture of their long-term vision. Far too often, people allow external circumstances to dictate their career paths. They might accept roles that "come along at the right time" or make career decisions based upon utilizing a specific degree that offers immediate stability and convenience, without fully exploring whether that path aligns with their long-term dreams and their broader vision for their future.

> ## A future vision is not just a career goal; it's a guiding principle that shapes every decision and opportunity along one's professional journey. It's the difference between passively reacting to opportunities and proactively driving toward a dreamy job.

The concept of a future vision requires individuals to articulate what they truly want from their lives and careers—not just in terms of titles or salary, but in terms of impact, fulfillment, and personal growth. A future vision becomes a compass, helping individuals evaluate opportunities and make decisions that consistently move them closer to their ultimate life–work goals.

One of the most significant barriers to developing a future vision is the misconception that it must be perfectly defined and fixed. A future vision should evolve as individuals gain new experiences, insights, and clarity about their values and passions. The key is to create a starting point—a vision that is detailed enough to provide direction but flexible enough to adapt as circumstances change.

Equally important is the discipline to align every career move with this vision. This doesn't mean rejecting roles that don't seem like an exact fit; it means approaching each opportunity with a clear understanding of how it contributes to the bigger picture. Whether it is a job promotion or a lateral or geographical move, an unexpected opportunity is a stepping stone if it provides valuable skills, connections, or experiences that support the person's future vision.

Building a career around a future vision also helps individuals avoid the common pitfall of defining success solely through external metrics like promotions or financial gains. Instead, it encourages a more holistic approach that prioritizes personal fulfillment and long-term happiness. By staying focused on their future vision, professionals are more likely to achieve what can truly be described as a "dreamy job": a role that leverages their skills and attributes and resonates deeply with their sense of purpose and passion.

DEFINING A PERSON'S FUTURE VISION

Skills and attributes can be taught and learned; future vision cannot. All three should be part of a hyper-individualized development plan.

In an organization, skill and attribute gaps are identified through surveys and management input. Training and development plans are then used to improve that person's skills and attributes, helping them to perform at a higher level and preparing them for promotions.

Future vision, however, has a much different learning pathway. Experiences and exposure inform future vision. There are abundant examples that illustrate this concept, such as an inner city youth discovering that a career in marine biology exists when they see the ocean for the first time or a youth raised on the ocean discovering they can become an apartment building manager when they visit a metropolitan city for the first time.

In a professional context, potentially life-changing learning that helps to inform a person's future vision is achieved by exposing contributors to different functions and departments within an organization. Mentorships, cross-functional job shadowing or job sharing, and rotational training programs are three of many ways that contributors can be exposed to many different experiences within the organization.

In summary, having a dream job is done by acquiring the skills and attributes that support a future vision.

While Gen Z has less professional experience, its members are also thoughtful and smart. They don't expect perfection; they expect progress.

BARB'S STORY

The day I met Barb, we sat staring at a cold slide presentation lying between us on the even colder twenty-foot-long marble-topped boardroom table. This deck of perfected pages outlined her organization's people strategy.

The CEO had asked me to develop a strategy that would ensure her connection with her young workforce and build a long-term corporate legacy. However, the slides only outlined financial, tax, and legal constructs related to a skills-based training plan. Nothing addressed the emotional themes that matter most to young professionals. She hadn't addressed attributes or future vision.

> Contributors with high emotional well-being are the most loyal, high-performing contributors.

I swiftly scanned the deck and pointed out, "If your mission is to build a loyal, highly motivated workforce, then let's address attributes and future vision to create a sub-strategy of your people strategy that specifically addresses your young professionals."

As we went on to develop this strategy, the CEO realized that while the work we were doing targeted young people, it applied to all of her workforce. The strategy boosted morale and leadership skills throughout all generations.

> When a young professionals strategy is well conceived, it turns into an all-generations people strategy because you've achieved your goal: keeping your contributors for a lifetime. Eventually Gen Z will be the "older generation."

INVISIBLE ATTRIBUTES

I began my next career journey as a chief legacy officer supporting an ultra-high-net-worth (UHNW) individual and his family. The goal of my work was to ensure that every member of the family had a plan for defining their purpose in life and a pathway to achieve it.

Through that work, I became aware that the younger generations were the most confused about how to define and achieve their potential. The younger generations were focused on having life–work balance and life goals but unclear on how to create a life plan to reach those goals. Throughout my years of mentoring and advising young entrepreneurs, I frequently observed this pattern of lacking a clear plan. Simply put, they have big dreams and no idea how to reach them.

This is how my work of helping organizations support their Gen Z contributors was born. The same tenets of helping young legacy family members apply to young professionals. They too require a blueprint for going from where they are to where they want to be. Most young people are clear on the education and skills they need to obtain to get a job, but they don't understand that there are other critical, invisible attributes that are even more powerful in helping them progress upward in their careers.

Throughout my career, I have worked with and become a confidante, mentor, and friend to members of the C-Suite, board members, founders, innovators, self-made high-net-worth-individuals (HNWIs), and people at all levels of executive leadership. All have consciously developed their invisible attributes.

Many started in the lowest level of the organization. They stocked shelves, served burgers, worked the assembly line, or sorted the mail room. They drove in a duct-taped car to a job they didn't like much. When they got to work, they asked questions, made and acknowledged mistakes, observed colleagues, and asked for help. They always volunteered for more responsibility and assignments, never shirking from hard work and discipline.

I've become a superfan of these people. They now navigate highly stressful roles that drive the economy, feed the world, move political outcomes, and catapult global innovation.

These leaders do all of that while fielding questions and criticisms from people who don't have complete knowledge and understanding about their businesses. Without inside knowledge, people make armchair comments, publicizing and politicizing negative, often inaccurate information to garner attention and support for their own causes. The leaders powerfully lead and march forward through the volatile environmental changes brought by negative media, boycotts, disasters of many forms, shutdowns, competition, laws and tax regulations, and the fickle consumers' changing tastes and beliefs.

And most importantly, great leaders do all of this while supporting, leading, guiding, and nurturing their organization's most important asset: their talent. After intense work, they go home at night and become Mom, Dad, son, brother, partner, and friend. They work on weekends, work on vacations, and spend evenings in their home offices after their families have turned in for the night.

Then they rise before dawn to return to the office with an appropriate and calculated mix of powerful, empathetic, and decisive leadership. Many great leaders conquered each progressive role without formal on-the-job training, making decisions on matters they had never encountered before, without any precedent guiding them—decisions that moved the economy, impressed or depressed their workforce, and put them in the crosshairs of competition, media, and the public.

While most choose their career paths and obtain appropriate formal education and technical skills to achieve their career goals, the thing that separates all great leaders is their unseen, invisible attributes. Leaders aren't educated about managing job pressures, having charisma, or being fully prepared for a role that changes daily. Instead, they use their invisible attributes to lead organizations.

In previous generations, these invisible attributes were thought to be hardwired. People frequently use the term *born leader* to indicate a person's innate ability to lead and manage others. The roles at the highest level of organizations are regularly secured because attributes like confidence, critical thinking, and adaptability were used as a means of selection. But at the lower levels of an organization, hiring is based primarily on education and skills, not attributes—even though attributes are an equally important measure of predicting success and high performance.

Today, we know that attributes can be either innate or learned and developed. A person may be a "born leader" or a "developed leader." Both types require mature and robust invisible attributes.

INVISIBLE ATTRIBUTES

The list of invisible attributes could be unending. The ones below are some that I use to build professional developmental strategies in the workforce. Depending on the role, different attributes may be required for success. Attention to detail, for example, is a tremendous attribute for project managers. Still other attributes—accountability, for instance—extend to all roles.

Resilience
Adaptability
Self-discipline
Time management
Emotional intelligence
Self-awareness
Accountability
Problem-solving skills
Communication skills
Leadership abilities
Decision-making skills
Work ethic
Creativity
Attention to detail
Teamwork
Positive attitude
Patience
Empathy
Confidence
Conflict resolution skills
Goal setting
Stress management
Open-mindedness
Integrity
Continuous learning
Networking skills
Perseverance
Negotiation skills
Flexibility
Critical thinking

While organizations often place my work under the diversity, equity, and inclusion umbrella, I view it as the next generation of DEI. It's a hyper-individualized approach that doesn't place people into groups; it removes them from groups and focuses on the unique individual.

APPLICANT TRACKING SYSTEM (ATS)

ATS refers to the software used by human resource talent acquisition teams to narrow down, reject, or accept an applicant for the next step of hiring for a role. Most companies, including 99 percent of Fortune 500 companies, now use ATS software to rank and filter job applicants. Uniqueness, creativity, and individual attributes are not considered at this stage of the hiring process by organizations that use ATS. ATS values word conformity, word monotony, and skill homogeneity and removes unique candidates—a serious flaw in this recruiting methodology and one that defies wisdom.

HR teams use ATS for efficiency, as this technology can review far more résumés in a short time than a human can. While ATS is designed to operate without personal bias or opinion, it still has inherent technological biases. For example, if the ATS is programmed to search for the word *creative* and an applicant uses the word *imaginative* instead, the résumé may be rejected even though the applicant possesses the desired quality. The purpose of ATS is to select candidates who have included the necessary search terms on their résumé and doesn't account for different interpretations of descriptors like *creative*.

Because of this process, résumés are rarely written to contain emotional or values-based attributes. As a result, candidates with strengths in soft skills, empathy, emotional intelligence, and unique life experiences can be overlooked, despite these invisible attributes being crucial for success in the role and effective future leadership. Attributes that may be overlooked include values, habits, beliefs, heritage, lifestyle, thinking styles, and personality, among others.

DEI initiatives have proven the value and importance of including a wide range of perspectives in business decision-making. We know that including the insight of people from varied backgrounds improves creativity and expands organizations' addressable market. Incorporating DEI into corporate strategies is not just a moral imperative but also a strategic advantage that drives better business outcomes and fosters a more dynamic, inclusive, and equitable workplace.

Inherited DEI traits are an advantage that support the success of an organization. Factors such as ethnicity, religion, gender, age, and socioeconomic designations offer a wide range of perspectives that could otherwise be overlooked. However, even if ATS accounted for inherited attributes, these traits wouldn't fully capture a person's attitudes, thinking, aspirations, values, or beliefs. They might give a general sense of who the person is, but no two people are the same, regardless of their inherited attributes.

To build inherited attributes and improve business outcomes even more, invisible attributes need to be incorporated into the HR processes. An example of this is a candidate of color who was born in a rough neighborhood of New York City. They inherited many attributes that inform their current thinking, behaviors, and attitudes and make them special. That person may also have attributes that provide strong leadership and decision-making skills, such as resilience, hard work, and an awareness of others. These are invisible, but powerful. While it's not appropriate to generalize about what invisible attributes this upbringing taught the candidate, it stands to reason that there are many special attributes that they possess.

When an organization begins to account for learned, inherited, and invisible attributes, they will flourish in many ways, including the following:

- Enhanced innovation and creativity: Teams bring together different perspectives, ideas, and problem-solving approaches, which can lead to more innovative solutions and creative thinking.

- Improved decision-making: A variety of viewpoints lead to thorough and well-rounded decision-making processes. Broad-thinking teams are better equipped to identify potential risks and opportunities from multiple angles.

- Better financial performance: Research has shown that companies with varied leadership styles often outperform their competitors. This performance includes higher revenue growth, greater market share, and more profitability.

- Attraction of top talent: A company's commitment to developing attributes can make it more attractive to job seekers, particularly those in Gen Z, whose members prioritize inclusive workplaces. This helps with attracting and retaining top talent from a broader pool.

- Enhanced employee engagement and retention: When employees feel valued, respected, and included, specifically for their uniqueness, they are more likely to be engaged and satisfied with their work. This leads to higher productivity, lower turnover rates, and a more positive work environment.

- Broader market reach: New ideas in the workforce can serve a diverse customer base, leading to new market opportunities.

- Compliance and risk management: Respecting unique backgrounds and perspectives helps companies comply with legal and regulatory requirements related to discrimination and equal opportunity. This reduces the risk of legal issues and reputational damage.

- Social responsibility and reputation: Demonstrating a commitment to individuality enhances a company's reputation and brand image. It shows that the company values fairness, equality, and social responsibility, which can strengthen relationships with stakeholders, including customers, investors, and the community.

- Reflection of global and local demographics: As businesses operate in increasingly global markets, reflecting the diversity of those markets within the organization is essential for relevance and competitiveness.

Technology has improved efficiencies but lost the human element of talent acquisition. The qualities that Gen Z in particular values highly, uniqueness and authenticity, are undervalued in today's recruiting technology.

HIRING GEN Z BASED ON SKILL IS A DEAD END

Gen Z are skilled. They have learned skills and formal techniques to solve problems. What makes them unique is their attributes. What attracts them to jobs is the contribution and life–work balance those jobs will provide.

Because Gen Z's overarching life goal is to protect their emotional, physical, and mental well-being, they search for a career that aligns with their values and lifestyle choices. Yet in 2024, according to the Sales Education Foundation, over 50 percent of Gen Z graduates from all majors begin their professional careers in entry-level sales roles,[6] and "over 60% of first-time salespeople fail within a year."[7] Failure at their first professional role does not get Gen Z excited about joining the workforce.

The high failure rate suggests that young adults are starting their professional lives in roles they have the technical skills for, the ones the HR applicant tracking software shows are present. But ATS hiring ignores the candidate's invisible attributes, such as temperament, personality, attention to detail, and communication skills. Yet using those attributes is essential for a Gen Z contributor to be happy, to be motivated, and to excel in the role. It's no wonder they leave and have negative associations with corporate roles.

The hard financial impact of this style of hiring is staggering in terms of numbers. Consider that the 1.2 million graduates who will be recruited, trained, and turned over within one year costs the US roughly $50 million. The hidden costs of a candidate's time and emotional well-being are incalculable.

Many Zoomers are well aware that the sales role is not a perfect role for them, so they plan their exit strategies before they begin day one of their new positions. They use the entry-level role as a résumé builder and as a means of getting their foot in the door. For organizations, a moral imperative and fiscally responsible way to hire is by identifying the emotional and invisible attributes of candidates.

6   Sales Education Foundation, "Who We Serve," accessed May 30, 2025, https://salesfoundation.org/who-we-serve.
7   Sales Education Foundation, "Key Statistics on Professional Sales Education," 2023, https://salesfoundation.org/wp-content/uploads/2024/07/2023-key-stats-sales-education.pdf.

YOUNG PROFESSIONALS STRATEGY: PROFILE THE ROLE

Hidden Costs of Poor-Quality Entry-Level Job Postings

There is an alarming trend in job postings that state that entry-level roles require several years of experience. This undermines your hiring process and costs millions in acquisition costs:

- True first-time, entry-level candidates don't feel they have the experience to land the role they went to college to obtain. As it relates to their role, they start their careers with an emotional bank account that's in the negative.

- Young people will take "any role to get their foot in the door." They begin searching for the next role soon after accepting the current one, which forces your company to backfill their position. They will make this decision before starting, and it is very difficult to change their minds.

> Many organizations reuse job postings for roles, even though they didn't result in long-term hires the first time, entering into a hiring tornado of wasted time, energy, and money.

This job posting is based on a real entry-level job posting that is vague, unemotional, and does little to accurately identify the right candidate for the role.

```
Join our team of Digital Advisors in empower-
ing our clients to understand, analyze, and
expand their business for optimal growth. By
skillfully creating strategic road maps, opti-
mizing and automating processes, and adeptly
managing change at project and organizational
levels, we build paths to success together
with our clients. Our unique approach departs
```

from conventional system integration methods, nurturing collaborative partnerships and fostering transformative outcomes.

As experienced Management Consultants, we carry the burden of visualizing the big picture and mapping out sustainable trajectories toward solutions. Leveraging our symbiotic collaboration with a variety of Service Units in our company, we coordinate a balanced amalgamation of knowledge, topical know-how, and business intelligence. Adhering to the tenet of client centricity, we deliver measurable, concrete value with steadfast commitment. Join us in molding the future of industry via innovation, cooperation, and the persistent pursuit of excellence.

These two paragraphs are word salad and could be used in *any* job posting at *any* company.

Support Change Strategy Implementation: Offer the development and execution of change management strategies and plans to help employees adopt new processes, tools, and technologies.

Stakeholder Engagement: Work closely with project teams and client stakeholders to gather input, understand concerns, and ensure alignment throughout the change process.

Impact Analysis: Conduct change impact assessments to determine the extent of changes and recommend appropriate actions.

Communication and Training Support: Help create and deliver communication materials and training programs that support the transition and enhance end-user adoption.

> Risk Identification: Identify resistance to change and propose strategies to mitigate risk.
>
> Data Gathering and Reporting: Track and measure the effectiveness of change management activities, providing insights and reports to project teams.
>
> Leadership and Team Support: Provide support to project leaders and ensure all team members are informed and aligned on the change objectives.

These bullets are too general in nature—they need more detail. For example, what does the contributor truly do to "offer the development and execution of change management strategies"? What does "gather input" mean: Will this candidate be analyzing spreadsheets or interviewing clients? Those two ways of gathering information require vastly different skills and attributes.

This client's rewritten job posting was successful in mapping candidates with the role by including the emotional and career development path within the role. It is a revision of a posting for the same role, but indicates a better work environment and age-appropriate skills, attributes, and future vision for an entry-level role.

> **Step into Transformation:**
> **Join Our Digital Advisory Team**
>
> Are you ready to jump into a role where you'll help industries adapt, grow, and find new ways to thrive? Our Digital Advisory Team is looking for fresh thinkers ready to dive into impactful work. Here, we're all about making big ideas happen for clients in the mobility and manufacturing sectors. Whether it's mapping out new strategies, fine-tuning processes, or guiding teams through change, you'll be a crucial part of driving success for our clients.

This is an inspiring post. It informs the potential candidate that they will be respected for their thinking and will have an impact on the business.

> **Who We Are and What You'll Do**
>
> As part of our team, you'll work side-by-side with experienced management consultants who see the big picture and will mentor and teach you how to build your own view. We bring together expertise across different areas of management, including finance, marketing, operations, and sales, to create collaborative solutions that actually make a difference. You don't have to know everything on day one. Our team is here to support and guide you.

This paragraph tells the potential candidate that they will be developed and cared for by seasoned associates and that they will learn about the other business units of the organization. It indicates they will be developed—a key request of Gen Z.

> **What Your Day-to-Day Could Look Like**
>
> Support Change Strategy Implementation: Learn the ropes of creating change strategies that help teams adjust to new tools and ways of working, making change smoother for everyone involved.
>
> Stakeholder Engagement: Collaborate with clients and project teams to listen, understand needs, and make sure everyone stays on the same page through the process.
>
> Impact Analysis: Assist in assessing the effects of changes, helping the team recommend the best next steps.
>
> Communication and Training Support: Be part

of developing materials that make it easier for end users to adapt, from creating helpful guides to planning training sessions.

Risk Identification: Spot potential bumps in the road and learn strategies to overcome them.

Data Gathering and Reporting: Track the effectiveness of changes and bring unique insights to help us all learn and improve.

Leadership and Team Support: Work closely with project leaders, helping keep the team aligned and informed as you support meaningful change.

If you're ready to bring your curiosity, collaboration skills, and enthusiasm to a team that's all about driving meaningful change, we'd love to hear from you! Come make your mark with us, build your skills, and start shaping the future of industry, one step at a time.

This section goes a long way in explaining the day-to-day role. It allows candidates to align their strengths with the role and come to the interview prepared to explain *why* they would map to the role.

During the interview, the candidate can provide clear examples of how they align with the position, and the interviewer can assess if their skills and attributes will truly align with the role.

THE INTERVIEW

When interviewing candidates, ensure these determinants of success are met:

1. Technical skills that clearly match the knowledge and capabilities required for the role. Review transcripts and other certificates of skills to ensure the candidate meets minimum skill requirements.
2. Individual attributes that identify the personality and emotional strengths of people best suited for each role. Ask the candidates for examples in their lives that illustrate whatever attribute you are interested in.

3. Transparency about the day-to-day work required in the role. As I mentioned, Gen Z will assess the role during onboarding, and if they feel the role is not what was described in the posting and interview, they will leave. There is a compelling advantage to being transparent about what the role truly entails.

Eighty-seven percent of the one hundred young professionals I interviewed who were in their first roles for three months said they had not understood what the day-to-day job would involve and had been too afraid to ask because they didn't want to appear uninformed about the role and didn't want to put off the interviewer. Most of the 13 percent who'd understood the day-to-day role had a relative or good friend already in the role who'd informed them. Sixty percent of respondents said they were disappointed in the day-to-day activities they were asked to do.

Use Attributes to Identify Candidates

The nursing industry readily illustrates the importance of aligning attributes with a role. Most of us agree that empathy is one of the most critical attributes in high-performing nurses. Hospitals and other health care organizations simply will not hire a nurse who lacks empathy.

In contrast, a sports science graduate, for example, may not have the attributes a top-performing nurse requires, even though they may share similar anatomy and health science knowledge.

Organizations that hire with a focus on mapping attributes to roles will have loyal high-performing associates.

THE IMPORTANCE OF ONBOARDING FOR LOYALTY

Gen Z place high expectations on their workplace experience, and quality onboarding is key to their long-term success. They want meaningful work, growth opportunities, and a sense of belonging from day one. Without it, they struggle to see how their roles fit the bigger picture, which leads to disengagement and higher turnover. Gen Z are making decisions about their future with organizations during onboarding—that's how important it is to have a good process.

Gen Z thrive on clarity and purpose. Members of Gen Z want to know how their contributions impact the organization's goals and need a structured introduction to the company's mission, culture, and expectations. Without this foundation, they can misinterpret the importance of their roles or feel disconnected from the team. Onboarding is the organization's chance to address these gaps and set a strong precedent for collaboration, inclusion, and growth.

However, onboarding isn't just about orientation sessions or paperwork. Gen Z expect onboarding to be personalized and interactive, with clear steps that outline how they'll succeed in their roles. They also look for opportunities to build relationships early on through mentorship programs or cross-functional introductions. If these elements are missing, Gen Z employees may question their value in the workplace and lose motivation quickly.

In addition, Gen Z place a high value on inclusion. A good onboarding program helps new hires feel welcomed and appreciated by emphasizing the organization's commitment to an open-minded, respectful workplace. For the Gen Z cohort, it's not just about filling out paperwork or learning policies—it's about building connections and understanding the value they bring to the team.

Gen Z employees may feel disconnected or undervalued without proper onboarding, leading to higher turnover rates. Organizations that invest in comprehensive onboarding improve retention and set the stage for long-term success by empowering young employees to thrive.

Steps to Successful Ongoing Onboarding

1. Pre-Onboarding: Begin onboarding before the new hire's first day. Don't surprise them; send them welcome videos and emails with details about what to expect, a schedule for their first week,

a day-in-the-life diary video, and any necessary paperwork. Provide access to digital resources, such as company handbooks or introductory videos, to help them feel prepared and informed. Stick to essential information; overwhelming Gen Z with extra details or, worse, humble-bragging, will quickly push them away.

2. Warm Welcome on Day One: Create a positive first impression by welcoming new employees warmly. Assign a mentor or buddy to guide them through the initial stages, and make sure their mentor connects on day one. Ensure their workstation is ready, and include a welcome package with useful items like branded merchandise or a personalized note.

3. Orientation and Culture Introduction: Introduce new hires to the company's mission, values, and culture through engaging presentations or videos. Highlight the organization's commitment to inclusion, teamwork, and professional development. Most importantly, help them understand how you intend on incorporating *their* values and career goals into their development plan. This step is critical for members of Gen Z, who seek workplaces that align with their values and future vision.

4. Role-Specific Training: Provide a detailed training curriculum outlining how you intend to personalize their development plan. Explain your use of AI, technology, and interactive and digital tools to make their learning process engaging and accessible.

5. Organization Training: Over the course of months, train your contributors on each organization's function. This means how each functional area operates, how they are incentivized, and best practices to interact with and impact each of the other business functions. Help them understand that excellent leaders understand the entire organization's landscape.

6. Financial Training: During your ongoing onboarding, make sure your contributors understand how to read *and interpret* their organization's public financial reports.

7. Cross-Functional Exposure: Arrange for new hires to meet with other departments and team leaders. This helps them understand the organization's structure and how different functions work together. Explain how your long-term training program includes interaction with and exposure to other departments. Gen Z value transparency and context, so showing its members the bigger picture is key.

8. Continuous Feedback: Design specific, clear, and logical key performance indicators. Schedule regular check-ins to provide constructive feedback and address any concerns. Gen Z thrives on clear communication and appreciates real-time feedback that helps them improve and grow.

9. Hyper-Personalized Development: Ongoing onboarding continues for the contributor's lifetime. Introduce the idea of hyper-personalized training and development programs and explain how you plan to create one for each contributor.

10. Career Ownership: Explain the importance of your employees owning their own career path and how you will support and train them to be their own advocates. This includes teaching them why and how to network both inside and outside of the organization, understanding role profiles at least two levels above the one for which they are being hired, and teaching them the critical skills required to build a path to their future vision.

By focusing on these steps, organizations can create an onboarding process that resonates with Gen Z, builds loyalty, and sets the foundation for a productive and fulfilling career.

When done well, ongoing onboarding fosters engagement and retention. Gen Z employees, who initially may not understand how their work impacts the organization, begin to see their value and align with the company's mission. By prioritizing onboarding as a way to connect the dots for young professionals—highlighting how decisions and roles interconnect—organizations can build a workforce that is informed, motivated, and ready to contribute meaningfully to long-term success. This intentional approach not only meets Gen Z's expectations, it also creates a foundation for stronger collaboration, innovation, and loyalty across the company.

CAREER OWNERSHIP: FOCUS ON INDIVIDUALS, NOT PEOPLE

Too many contributors offload their careers to a manager and then complain when they don't achieve their goals.

> Forty-six percent of employees say their manager doesn't know how to help them with their career development. So teach contributors to own their careers.

How can an organization focus on every person within the organization and ensure that everyone is getting what they need? By using a framework for discovery, assessment, training, and *personal* ongoing career management. As organizational leaders, you are uniquely positioned to incorporate this framework.

A commonly heard phrase among health care providers and the public is "Own your health care journey." This phrase emphasizes the importance of taking an active and informed role in managing one's health. This means being proactive about seeking medical advice, understanding treatment options, making lifestyle changes, and staying informed about one's health status. By owning one's health care journey, individuals can make more informed decisions, advocate for themselves, and ultimately achieve better health outcomes.

This is the same advice I give Gen Z and organizations regarding contributor development. For decades, contributors have consistently trusted their careers to their managers in the same way many people have trusted their health care to a doctor or health care system. In the workplace, if a contributor didn't reach their career expectations, they readily blamed their manager, HR, or another organizational entity. According to one survey conducted by INTOO, almost half of Gen Z believe they get better career advice from a chatbot than from their managers. And 62 percent of Gen Z associates say they want to talk to their manager more about their career, but their manager is too busy for such conversations.[8]

I encourage everyone, not just Gen Z, to own their own career development and to use their managers as mentors, guides, or coaches—but not as the owners and orchestrators—of their career development. Contributors have to take ownership themselves to assure they are doing what is needed to achieve optimal success.

Three out of four contributors, not just in Gen Z, believe they have received poor development advice from their managers. There are several reasons for this, including the fact that managers often don't have time to manage every team member and aren't trained in career development. Managers can't possibly know their contributors' inner hopes and dreams—only contributors can see that for themselves. Whether or not managers genuinely lack the ability to help, Gen Z can address the issue by taking ownership of their career development.

And they should! This is why companies that train contributors and managers to own their own careers will succeed in the future. With 60 percent of contributors claiming their employers don't care or take time to help them search for roles outside their current department, it is crucial to teach contributors to map their own plans before going to their managers for support.

Giving Gen Z the Tools They Need

By emphasizing that they should use their own data, you assure Gen Z that they are not being placed on a standard, one-size-fits-all career path. Instead, their data informs their individual career path. Contributors are taught to use their personal data, with specific and identifiable metrics they have chosen, to take ownership of their own professional and personal growth.

In one organization, this personal ownership resulted in the reengagement and swapping of team members who found they were not utilizing their greatest skills but could do so by mapping their capabilities to the role profiles within other functional areas of the organization. In essence, the team members discovered that their passion-driven capabilities and attributes were better suited to different roles. When they transitioned to the new functions, their performance and SWB improved.

---

8   INTOO, "Unlocking Organizational Success Report," 2024, https://resources.intoo.com/featured-content/intoo
    -unlocking-organizational-success-report-2024.

> If you choose only one thing to do to train upcoming leaders, choose to teach them *how* to own their own career.

TERRIN'S STORY

Terrin is a unique member of Gen Z; he discovered his career passion, commercial real estate, during college. Though his degree was not in real estate, he committed himself to getting his license during college, worked in a real estate office during the school year, and took unpaid summer internships to learn the business.

Though he had more experience than his graduating peers, Terrin did not expect to get a higher-level role than any of his colleagues. Instead, he accepted an entry-level role and proved himself time and again to be a high-performing contributor.

In a fast-paced, high-stress industry, Terrin didn't wait for his HR team to manage his career development plan and outline his career path. Terrin started keeping track of his career with a spreadsheet. He identified his ultimate role in real estate and added a target date to reach that position.

Then he used the outcome-first approach to identify the steps that would bring him to that ultimate role. The columns along the top of the spreadsheet showed the essential skills and attributes he needed to gain throughout his career. He labeled the rows with the promotions he needed to earn along the way. For each role, he identified a specific course, workshop, mentorship, network opportunity, or association membership to help him build that skill or attribute. Some goals, like joining an industry association, he recognized as ongoing career builders. Others were one-time training programs. All had target dates of completion.

He continued to excel at work, and while he wasn't high enough in the organizations to own a portion of the deals he worked on, his teams always showed him that they valued him in other ways. He received large bonuses each year, many small dinner gift certificates, and, once, a fully paid airplane ticket for two, to use in any way he wished.

It's been six years since graduation, and Terrin has switched roles three times in order to stay on his development plan. Leadership recognizes Terrin as a high-potential contributor, and each career move has been endorsed and recommended by mentors within his organization.

Terrin has never burned a bridge but has been consistently honest, asking for guidance, coaching, and support from his colleagues, managers, and leadership. Most of all, he has managed his career development and been true to himself.

This story is meaningful because people often accuse Gen Z of leaving roles too soon. Terrin moved frequently but was fully transparent with his leaders about why he was going. When he did that, his organization supported him. They understood he needed to move to get the experience he needed to reach his ultimate goal. The most essential lesson that can be learned from Terrin's story is that Gen Z must be encouraged to own their career development and career path.

ENGAGING FOR LIFE

Commitment to contributors from pre-hiring to the last day of their employment pays for itself in several ways:

1. It eliminates the hard costs associated with attracting and hiring.
2. It creates a natural succession plan that ensures your organization trains the next generation of workforce and promotes their career development and future vision.
3. It boosts competencies among your workforce. (Remember, people like to do what they are good at and perform better when they feel highly qualified.)
4. It improves morale throughout your organization because people who feel valued not only perform better, but are also more likable, and other contributors like to work with them.

HR Team Benefits from Contributor Talent Panning

Most HR professionals are motivated and inspired by the growth and development of the talent they support. Human resource teams benefit when they create efficient, cost-effective programs to assist them in individualizing recruiting, development, and engagement plans.

HR teams that embrace a modern, technology-forward process for understanding the individuals within their workforce emerge with streamlined programs that support their teams across the talent lifecycle. This lifecycle engagement approach benefits everyone connected to your organization, including individual contributors, first-time managers, seasoned managers, executive leadership, the board of directors, shareholders, customers, and ultimately the global community.

Successful HR programs focus upon respect, contribution, and long-term personal and career growth. Measured and cost-effective programs designed to reward ideas, implement cross-departmental training and temporary role swapping, and identify best-in-class development plans for each contributor are discovering loyalty in their workforce. These programs are proven to be successful in recruiting and engaging associates.

There are also incredible unforeseen benefits that emerge. New, solid cross-generational relationships are built. Boomers, Gen Xers, millennials, and Gen Zers begin to share knowledge and innovation throughout the business.

Improvements Extend Across the Organization

First-time managers have a really tough job. These typically young managers are chosen because they excelled at their previous role. Unfortunately, they are often promoted prior to obtaining the skills they need to be a productive and inspiring manager.

In fact, in many cases, their prior success as individual contributors was predicated on their ability to achieve solitary goals, which can be in direct conflict with the collaborative nature of managerial responsibilities that are focused on team achievement and performance.

Like most people, many first-time managers have in the past gravitated toward like-minded coworkers, so learning about and leading a diverse group of individuals creates new challenges. These managers benefit by working for an organization that identifies the specific management leadership skills they need to emphasize in their career development plan in order to become effective and outstanding managers.

As managers, we have all taken generic training programs that didn't resonate with us personally. These programs wasted our time and frustrated us. We knew we had other areas we would like to have been trained in.

Organization-wide management training programs are no longer appropriate. Organizations need to identify the exact gaps in each management individual and train specifically for that person's gaps. As each invisible skill—such as confidence, resilience, empathy, and communication—is boosted, these managers will become higher-performing leaders throughout their careers. You will be helping them attain their career goal: to become an effective leader of high-performing teams.

CASSANDRA'S STORY

Cassandra has spent twenty years in the field of recruiting, supplying multiple industries with associates at all levels, from entry-level to CEO. She has seen the very best interviewees and the very worst. In Cassandra's mind, the worst come from Gen Z. She has witnessed that they have high demands from their employers and aren't shy about asking for what they want.

Her most significant issue is how they express these preferences in the first interview. She says, "They don't understand that they are important but another one hundred interviewees are vying for the same role." While she admires their interest in climbing the ladder, their eagerness for promotions without focusing on the job they're being interviewed for is insulting and offensive.

Gen Z's tendency to job-hop—with its members often quitting roles that don't meet their expectations, without a backup plan—can lead firms to prefer more experienced candidates, even for entry-level positions. "We are looking for people who aren't this entitled Gen Z–type of candidate," Cassandra said, noting that turnover is expensive.

According to Cassandra, the following are Gen Z's biggest mistakes:

- They don't research the company or the interviewer.

- They do not recognize that they have only one chance to impress their potential employer during an interview.

- They don't realize that they need to respect hierarchy, be willing to sacrifice some "perfect world" requests, and earn respect and benefits.

- They underestimate the importance of "executive presence" during their interviews.

Yet Cassandra has a mission to bring Gen Z to her clients' workforces, so she needs to solve her problem, which is that Gen Z are unprepared, are sometimes disrespectful, and appear cocky during their interviews. To help Cassandra solve the problem, we deployed a Recruiting and Interview Special Forces Team (RISFT). Her voluntary program helps candidates prepare for their interviews at the organization for which she is recruiting.

While the information is common knowledge to older generations, Gen Z are not learning basic professional skills while getting their education. The key to the RISFT is that Cassandra and her team supplement Gen Z's formal education with what they need to know to accelerate their careers.

Cassandra positions the program as a development program for young people so they know it will prepare them for the workplace, not give them free entry into the workforce. She doesn't tell them how to "get the job." Instead, she teaches them how to prepare, in order to increase their job chances. She teaches them how to network, how to prepare for the interview, what is appropriate to ask at an interview, and how to present themselves in the best light for the interview.

For example, the RISFT doesn't tell candidates how to dress. Instead, it teaches why people should care about their presence, that is: what an executive presence is and why it matters.

Her goal is not to change anyone or do the work for them; it's to teach candidates why they should care about things they didn't learn about in school and how to do the work themselves.

Don't forget the interns! Seventy percent of interns are hired at the same company they interned with following their internship.[9] Internships offer value to both the company and the individual contributor, providing the opportunities to gain deeper work relationships, improved training programs, holistic engagement, and a better understanding of each other.

---

9   Tom Jendriks, "105 Internship Statistics: Pay, Intern Employment, and Demographics," Flair, January 15, 2024, https://flair.hr/en/blog/internship-statistics.

In addition, Cassandra implemented an in-house internship program in her agency that she uses to help prepare young people for their first jobs by focusing on internships. She uses her internships to feed entry-level performers into her clients' organizations, and she considers it an entry-level succession plan for her clients.

To build her internship program, Cassandra followed the steps she deploys for her clients but focused on pre-entry-level Gen Z. She examined her organization's internship job profiles, job posts, and interviews for interns. In her internship program, she provides practical training to help interns prepare for the next stage of their lives.

Cassandra discovered that her numbers, like the national average, hovered at 70 percent of her interns returning the following year for additional development. They returned and were ready to contribute on day one because they had clear expectations and knowledge about their internship role.

> Cassandra's interns have been placed throughout her network of client organizations at a success rate of 100 percent upon college graduation. She places 100 percent of her interns in an entry-level role in the first semester of their senior year.

DEBUNKING THE MYTH

The myth about Gen Z says that they all want to work from home in a dream job. It is true that members of Gen Z expect a lot from their careers, but they understand that having a dream job is not easy. They are willing to put in the time if they are clear that they have a plan to help them develop into their most productive selves. They will gladly own the management of that plan—they like to have ownership.

What Should You Do?

Hard and soft skills are important for career progression, but they don't guarantee success.

FOCUS ON INHERENT ATTRIBUTES

Inherent attributes can be learned, groomed, and boosted. For example, some children show greater empathy than their classmates from the onset of their lives. Other children need to learn empathy.

Even if two people follow the same educational path, acquire the same learned skills, and come from the same family, their invisible attributes will be unique. No two people have the exact same combination of invisible attributes. But the good news is that attributes that make a person truly valuable and unique, and that bring fresh ideas, can be taught.

Building robust attributes is critical to boosting a person's well-being. People who use their invisible gifts feel more peaceful and balanced, and happier, than those who work in roles that don't leverage their gifts. Envision a creative individual who works in accounting, never using their creativity and becoming painfully unmotivated. We have all heard the phrase, "Do what you love, and the money will come." There's truth to that adage in our context when *do what you love* means to use invisible attributes.

Improving individual well-being motivates and nurtures loyal, innovative, high-performing, high-quality contributors and leaders. Neglecting to focus on this part of contributors will leave employees feeling empty, and attracting and retaining them will be challenging and costly.

It is never too late to pick up a great new attribute. For some reason people have embraced the idea that attributes are genetic. People believe leaders are born, people either have confidence or they don't, empaths are naturally gifted in that way, and so on—that is simply untrue. People learn daily, particularly when they put effort into it.

With age comes wisdom, but you don't need to wait until you are old to learn new attributes.

HOW TO DETECT AND MEASURE ATTRIBUTES

Organizations begin by measuring their contributors' attributes. A set of questions are provided, and the responses are analyzed and serve as a baseline to inform two areas: (1) the organization's aggregate employee attribute strengths and (2) the strength of each individual's attributes.

Many attributes can be expected to be found within particular organizations. For example, a nonprofit whose contributors work tirelessly to support a common cause tends to score higher on empathy than a global financial institute. But the majority of organizations show a less obvious result when their full contributor population is measured on invisible attribute strengths and weaknesses. This information informs future function-specific or corporate-wide training programs. For example, an organization that identifies a weakness in detail orientation within their project management teams would want to train for that attribute.

The following table provides examples of questions that can help identify apparent attributes. To achieve the best results with attribute testing, organizations should align attributes and questions with specific job functions. This helps them to understand which attributes within that function need to be enhanced.

ATTRIBUTES AND QUESTIONS

Attribute being measured	Question key: Ensure questions are neutral and don't lead respondent to "wish" or "want" to answer a certain way.
Resilience	I consistently maintain focus on my goals despite encountering obstacles.
Reframing	I often recognize when my mental state is biased.
Problem-Solving	I seek out information that contradicts my initial hypotheses or beliefs.
Mindset: appropriate not always positive	I generally expect outcomes to be favorable, even in uncertain situations.
Confidence	I regularly question why I react the way I do in certain situations.
Self-reflection	When I experience a personal challenge, I take time to think about how it is an opportunity to learn about myself.
Consistency	I revise my values and principles to protect myself in my professional life.
Empathy and Emotional Intelligence	I can easily identify when someone feels sad or upset, even if they don't say anything.

Attribute being measured	Question key: Ensure questions are neutral and don't lead respondent to "wish" or "want" to answer a certain way.
Communication	I recognize and understand the nonverbal cues of others.
Conflict resolution	When a conflict arises, I prioritize finding a solution that satisfies all parties involved.
Self-awareness	I am aware of changes in my mood, thoughts, and behaviors.
Gratitude	I acknowledge effort and positive behaviors in others.
Selflessness	I help people out even if I don't personally benefit from my actions.
Leadership	I am always the kind of leader I admire.

USING ATTRIBUTES TO HIRE

By identifying the strength of individual's attributes, an organization can attract and retain the best contributors to fill each type of role. Remember that ATS system that uses skills-based keywords to identify potential candidates? Skills are the baseline, the minimum requirement that must have been learned if a candidate is to have the qualifications to fill a role. If, however, you want to find candidates that will excel long-term, include attributes on job postings and in ATS requirements.

Unfortunately, people can learn skills that suit a role perfectly and still not be the best for that role. This is made painfully clear in the insurance industry, which relentlessly hires from all backgrounds, majors, and geographies into their sales department. The insurance industry ranks among the lowest retention rates in the sales function of all industries. Their fatal flaw is that they hire Gen Z applicants using basic skill mapping but don't consider the attributes that make a contributor happy, loyal, and successful in their roles.

They use a traditional method of recruiting that relies upon hiring large numbers of entry-level associates, and they teach the contributors a "dialing for dollars" sales approach that relies on making a defined number of calls a day. What they don't recognize or communicate is that there is a clear "type" of person who excels and achieves high commissions. The majority of hires will leave within the first one to five years because they are left feeling that they aren't using their greatest strengths, their greatest attributes. In other words, they aren't doing what they love or what feeds their souls.

Some Gen Z contributors, however, learn that the fast-paced nature of the entry-level sales role is exciting and fun for them. In this case, knowing the attributes that develop strong sales professionals and matching those attributes with each contributor is a precise way of helping to develop contributors and helping them achieve great success in sales.

> "I don't to want be in sales, but I want a job and need to have something for my résumé. I know I won't like it. It doesn't even sound interesting, and I won't get to use my creativity enough."
> —M. J. M., Gen Z contributor and marketing major

THEY'RE TOO WOKE

I hear this characterization about Gen Z frequently: "They're too woke." Or put more gently, "They are overly sensitive."

Another word for woke is *aware*. Yes, they are very aware. As the most diverse generation in US history, they are very aware of the benefits, strengths, and weaknesses that come with different upbringings.

Reframing this awareness from a negative "woke" to a positive "awareness" is key to leveraging their unique ability to synthesize multiple opinions, perspectives, and cultures into their work.

Awareness is the modern way of saying you respect others.

SUBJECTIVE WELL-BEING: A MEASUREMENT (MOSTLY) OF HAPPINESS

Gen Z get a lot of heat for being vocal and animated about the emphasis they put on their emotional state. I want to reemphasize that they aren't suggesting they don't want robust careers. They just believe that a career doesn't need to come at the expense of their subjective well-being (SWB).

Subjective well-being measures a person's positive emotions, negative emotions, and life satisfaction, as reported by the person themselves. When most days, thoughts, feelings, and accomplishments are positive, SWB is positive.

A person should strive for "mostly"!

Traditionally, people used the word *happiness* to describe their ideal state, but subjective well-being is more encompassing and can be achieved more consistently than happiness. Subjective well-being was first described by Ed Diener, also known as "Dr. Happiness," a leading researcher in positive psychology, to account for emotional ups and downs.

Diener and others who have followed in his footsteps hypothesize that we are genetically predisposed to happiness as a defense mechanism for dealing with life's trials and tribulations. In normal functioning adults, that means a person can balance a negative emotional state with a genetically inherited positive disposition. In addition, people can supplement their genetic predisposition for happiness and other positive emotions with training and practice. In essence, a person can learn to acknowledge negative emotions and replace them with positive ones.

However, because everyone has unique life experiences, Dr. Happiness and others caution against making and applying conclusions across all populations. For our purposes, think of it this way: There are too many variables and measurement methods to conclude, without doubt, what programs positively impact your contributors' subjective well-being.

THE POWER OF "MOSTLY"

SWB is the measurement of positive emotions, negative emotions, and life satisfaction, as reported by the person themselves. When thoughts, feelings, and accomplishments are positive on most days, SWB is positive. Such a person is what I call "mostly."

Mostly is an important term in working with Gen Z because they tend to talk in absolute terms rather than recognizing there is a process to achieving balance and SWB. Gen Z want to be motivated, for example, but motivation isn't a sustainable construct—it fluctuates. The goal should be "mostly motivated." Similarly, Gen Z should strive for "mostly SWB."

That slight reframing would allow you to present this content as a strategy for achieving SWB and worker retention. It's important to teach Gen Z that achieving SWB is a journey, and "mostly" becomes a measurement tool HR actively uses to help their Gen Z employees work toward their personal versions of success.

The organization's issue becomes how to redesign the efficiencies of company-wide talent development programs to accommodate each employee's individual requirements. The advice "Don't build something for us without us" applies here perfectly. Using generative AI, traditional data analytics, and data shared by each employee, companies should teach Gen Z how to build their own SWB journey.

> ## Building and maintaining healthy relationships is fundamental to healthy human functioning, emotional well-being, and having a purpose in life.

Relationships and Subjective Well-Being (SWB)

Few things in life have greater potential to impact a person's positive emotions than solid relationships do. Strong relationships have almost zero downsides when managed well and can be practiced equally by people of all ages. But sadly, research shows that relationships, particularly across generations, are suffering at an increasing rate.

Degradation of family, social, and work relationships is impacting the mental well-being and emotional success of people. Relationships are undergoing a significant shift across the globe. "Those with poor family relationships and no close friends are ten times more likely to suffer from significant mental health challenges than those with many close family bonds and friendships and 53% of young adults rarely or never discuss their mental health with their parents."[10]

However, there is good news: The most recent Edelman Trust Barometer notes that "As today's societal issues continue to mount, employees now see their workplace as a safe space for debate and turn to it as a primary source of community—before their neighbors and religious organizations."[11] By creating ways to build relationships, your workplace can be an obvious choice for contributors seeking opportunities to enhance their well-being.

---

10   Sapien Labs, "The Mental State of the World in 2022: Friendships and Mental Wellbeing," March 1, 2023, https://sapienlabs.org/wp-content/uploads/2023/06/Friendships-and-Mental-Wellbeing.pdf.
11   Edelman Trust Institute, "2025 Edelman Trust Barometer," 2025, https://www.edelman.com/sites/g/files/aatuss191/files/2025-01/2025%20Edelman%20Trust%20Barometer_Final.pdf.

EMMA AND JAKE'S STORY

Emma and Jake, two Gen Z professionals in the marketing department of a consumer packaged goods company, found themselves constantly frustrated with their work. Emma, a data analyst, and Jake, a meticulous and analytical marketing assistant, often felt out of place in their respective roles.

Emma loved brainstorming and coming up with innovative ideas, but her job required her to spend most of her time analyzing market trends and numbers, which she found tedious. On the other hand, Jake thrived on dissecting data and identifying patterns, but his role required him to pitch new ideas and work closely with clients, which made him uncomfortable.

Their frustration was evident in their interactions with colleagues and managers, and it became a topic of discussion during a company training weekend. The weekend included a workshop on utilizing personal data to enhance job satisfaction and productivity. Employees were encouraged to assess their strengths, weaknesses, and preferences using a detailed survey and a personality test.

Emma's results showed high scores in creativity, communication, and collaboration, while Jake's scores reflected his strengths in analysis, attention to detail, and problem-solving. The facilitator suggested that employees discuss their results with their peers and managers to find ways to align their roles better with their strengths.

Emma and Jake sat down together during a break and shared their frustrations and insights from the workshop. As they talked, it became clear that each one's personality and strengths were better suited to the other's role. Emma's creative mind and love for client interaction seemed perfect for the marketing role's client-facing aspects. In contrast, Jake's analytical prowess and preference for solitary work seemed ideal for the data analytics position.

"I can't believe we didn't realize this sooner," Emma said, laughing. "We've been struggling because we're in the wrong roles."

The idea of swapping jobs was unconventional, but they decided to propose it to their managers. They prepared a detailed plan outlining how the swap would benefit the company by improving job satisfaction and productivity. Their managers, intrigued by the idea, agreed to a trial period to see how it would work out.

The transition wasn't without its challenges. However, Emma and Jake supported each other through the learning process, becoming each other's mentors and coaches. Their enthusiasm for their new roles was palpable.

As weeks passed, the positive impact of the swap became evident. Emma thrived in her new role, bringing a fresh perspective to the team's strategies and fostering stronger client relationships. Her creative problem-solving skills and ability to think outside the box helped the team develop innovative solutions to complex problems.

Meanwhile, Jake excelled as an analyst. His analytical skills enabled him to identify key market trends and create data-driven campaigns that resonated with target audiences. He found satisfaction in diving deep into the numbers and uncovering insights that informed the marketing strategy.

Their managers, impressed with the results, decided to make the job swap permanent. Emma and Jake's productivity soared, and their job satisfaction levels were higher than ever. They'd found roles that truly aligned with their strengths and passions, proving that a fresh perspective and a willingness to embrace change can lead to remarkable outcomes.

Emma and Jake's story became an inspiration within the company, encouraging others to consider their attributes and interests when seeking career fulfillment. They learned that owning their career paths and being open to unconventional solutions could lead to personal and professional growth.

JAMAL'S STORY

Jamal sat in the corner, a bit removed at team meetings. His arms were crossed, and he didn't contribute to conversations unless asked by name for his thoughts. Jamal was the go-to guy for specific breakdowns in the company's technology department and was kept busy in that specialized function. But his colleagues and managers had learned to walk a large circle around his desk and stopped asking about weekends and family.

Jamal had made it obvious to his coworkers that he was not interested in small talk or in making friends. Day after day, he came into his office, sat at his desk, and was left alone by others as much as he left them alone. During team meetings, training workshops, and events, however, his demeanor had a negative impact on his entire team. His emotions seemed to spread to others around him.

New managers came, ran the team, got promoted, and left Jamal undisturbed in his corner of the office. Jamal, after all, had more tenure than any of the managers or teammates in his department—who were they to try to change him now or to disrupt what was working well: his expertise in the critical area he dominated? Though he wasn't in a customer-facing role, customers asked for Jamal by name to address their questions, mentor their associates, and solve their technology issues. Many claimed Jamal was the reason they remained customers.

Eventually, the organization embarked on a new Talent Empowerment Program. The program was designed to allow associates to analyze their current state of emotions, identify the gaps in their invisible attributes, offer options and resources for addressing the gaps, and educate contributors on how to be their own advocates.

Jamal enthusiastically participated in the voluntary program. He submitted survey responses and attended and asked questions in workshops and in Lunch and Learns. Inherently analytical and data-minded, Jamal was quick to accept his personal data as accurate, though no one else would have used it to describe Jamal's personality; everyone on his past and present teams had him profiled incorrectly.

Incredibly, Jamal's learned and inherent attributes mapped him to a managerial role in his department. The role he was suited for, managing a team of engineers, was two levels up and had never been brought up as a career path for him by anyone in his organization. However, Jamal had been vocal for years about the fact that he felt he needed more growth; he felt too pigeonholed and wanted to broaden his skill set.

Yet his managers hadn't known what to do with Jamal, and Jamal hadn't known how to proceed without help. Colleagues, managers, and leaders all saw Jamal as a quiet, slightly antisocial genius, not a people manager. Now, however, Jamal had data to support the idea that he should at least be considered for a management position.

Psychologist Daniel Goleman contends that emotional intelligence (EI), or a person's emotional quotient (EQ), accounts for 67 percent of the necessary capabilities required for superior performance in leaders, and "matters twice as much as technical expertise."[12]

---

12   Daniel Goleman, *Emotional Intelligence*, 10th ed. (Bantam Books, 2007), 41.

Yet there were cautionary data points too. His human counterparts didn't believe he was suited for management. And his data analytics indicated he had an opportunity to develop a key attribute of exceptional leaders: emotional intelligence.

Emotional intelligence appeared as an opportunity for growth for Jamal to achieve his new career objective. And the company was committed to supporting him and helped him design a development curriculum plan that targeted building his EQ.

> Many people with high intelligence, particularly those in fields where analytics and precision are highly regarded, don't recognize their lack of emotional intelligence. Their strength lies in the ability to focus singularly on a specific area, while EI relies heavily on broad awareness of larger groups.

Over the next six months, Jamal participated in training programs designed to help him learn emotional intelligence skills. The company funded some of the training; Jamal invested in some of it himself.

Courses on self-awareness, self-regulation, social skills, and active listening topped the list on Jamal's development plan. It wasn't surprising that someone as intelligent as Jamal could complete the training satisfactorily, but the real surprise was yet ahead.

After a year, by his own self-description he felt like he was "a new person." He became noticeably social, entertaining colleagues and customers with the humor he'd always had but had never showed. His physical presence became warm and engaging, replacing the closed-off, arms-crossed version of himself he once had been. And his confidence as a team leader surfaced as he contributed during team meetings without being prompted. He then needed a chance to manage people and showcase his new attributes.

That was two years ago. Jamal is now managing a small team, is frequently invited to leadership collaborations, and is building relationships throughout the organization. But his greatest strength to the organization and to himself is his ability to identify and mentor others in the organization who remind him of his old self.

Jamal is not only a high-potential leader, he also nurtures and mentors the next generation of leaders. Additionally, he has traveled to the organization's satellite offices to share how the empowerment program changed his life; he has become the voice of owning your career development and identifying your strengths and weaknesses.

HELICOPTER MANAGERS

None of Jamal's successes would have happened without his company's commitment to investing in his subjective well-being (SWB) and to empowering him to take charge of his own future. Allowing associates the freedom for self-discovery, even if their path to success is nonlinear, will yield the benefits that a company and its associates seek.

Let's consider a parenting analogy: the infamous helicopter parent. A helicopter parent is one who is overly involved in their child's life, often to an excessive degree. They tend to hover over their children, closely monitoring and controlling various aspects of their lives, including their education, social interactions, and extracurricular activities. Helicopter parents often intervene in their children's problems, try to prevent them from facing challenges or failures, and make decisions on their behalf. This level of involvement can sometimes hinder the child's ability to develop independence, problem-solving skills, and resilience.

Many associates across multiple industries and functions have relied heavily, sometimes exclusively, on their employer to direct and manage their careers. Just as a person should manage and advocate for their own health care and a child should take some personal responsibility for their learning journey, contributors should manage and advocate for their own careers.

In Jamal's case, he independently found a direct path to advancing his SWB and career. However, sometimes associates will have a less straightforward journey to success—they may discover that the grass isn't greener elsewhere in the company. This, too, is a win for both the company and the associate, as it fosters growth and learning.

Organizations should assist instead of being the sole source of a person's SWB and development plan.

BAD IS NOT ALL BAD

By training contributors and managers in your organization to understand themselves, you're helping them reach their potential. When people experience subjective well-being and their internal world is in order, they are free to perform at a higher level at work and at home, build strong relationships, and pursue bigger goals.

I'm not suggesting that, by monitoring SWB, you strive for a Panglossian world for your associates: one that is excessively and unachievably optimistic. Hardships, downturns in business, coworker issues, and other negative events are not weaknesses in the organization. Facing negative events, like facing everything in life, is a way of learning and revising plans.

Feeling negative emotions is not a weakness. It is an important data point in discovery.

Most people know someone who claims their glass is "always half full." That's a red flag: not the "half full" part, the "always" part. Just as too much negative emotion is detrimental to overall SWB, so is too much positive emotion. Remember, the goal is balance. And managers recognize that people who experience a broad spectrum of emotions, negative and positive, also tend to bring exciting, unique ideas.

An effective way to ensure a balance of positive and negative emotions among associates is to teach them about themselves. That may sound crazy—people should already know themselves—yet most people don't know, or don't spend time reflecting on, their triggers for positive and negative emotions. By exposing people to techniques that measure their triggers—and by teaching them how to boost the positive triggers, reframe the negative triggers, and balance the two—organizations help Gen Z take control of their career development.

DEBUNKING THE MYTH

The myth about Gen Z says that they're too woke. Gen Z is incredibly aware of others' backgrounds and choices. This is a fantastic leadership trait and will serve your organization well. Consider having multiple perspectives a modern way of incorporating new ideas into your workforce.

> **Gen Z's innate awareness will help you identify unforeseen consequences of your business practices before they potentially cost money in reputation and lost sales.**

What Should You Do?
MEASURE AND TRACK SWB

Older populations suffer from role stagnation. In every organization you will find contributors who excelled in their roles at one time but have simply become stagnant and unmotivated to go above and beyond expectations—much like Sally, who you met earlier in the book. This is another scenario in which personal data can be used to promote career development.

It's not as difficult as it may seem to gather useful contributor data. AI, personal chatbots, and data analytics all readily define, measure, and track an individual's emotions and attributes.

There are three steps to measuring and tracking SWB. In most cases, keeping questionnaires simple and brief yields higher participation and—over time, with tracking—information that's equally instructive as that gathered in long psychological tests. Contributors are taught how to take the test, measure and track their results, and stay in the ownership positions of their SWB development journeys.

Step 1: Find each individual's baseline measure of SWB.

Step 2: Identify and rank the individual's primary dimensions of well-being.

Step 3: Track well-being, month over month.

Step 4: Use the data to build individual development plans for improving SWB.

By comparing their responses over time, contributors will notice improvements or declines in their subjective well-being (SWB) and identify their key SWB triggers. Understanding what triggers positive changes in their SWB gives contributors a compass for tracking progress and making impactful changes. This allows them to take charge of their SWB development paths.

> "The greatest happiness you can have is knowing that you do not necessarily require happiness." —William Saroyan

ORGANIZATIONS THAT CARE WILL RECEIVE CARE IN RETURN

When contributors take control of their SWB, they tend to make themselves available as better mentors and advisors to other contributors. This is particularly important for people managers. Consider the friends you have that are constantly negative. They become a drain on you and everyone around them, and they lack direction and purpose.

In contrast, an emotionally well-balanced person becomes a person whose positive influence rubs off on others—they have a positive impact on others. Along with positively influencing others, emotional balance ultimately allows people to move toward discovering their undiscovered contribution at work and purpose. Managers who are meant to be managers see that immediately; others may need training or a new role to make their best contribution.

Cooperative Growth

Many organizations subsidize contributors' health club memberships with the understanding that base level health is critical to their performance at work. But if the contributor wants to hire a personal trainer or coach to motivate and accelerate their fitness, they pay for that themselves.

Likewise, it's okay for organizations to subsidize a certain amount of contributor development and for contributors to contribute to some of their own development. The key, again, is communication and transparency.

In fact, many, many online workshops, videos, and community classes offer free or low-cost options for people who want to improve their personal skill set.

THEY LIVE FOR MENTAL HEALTH DAYS

Whether we agree or disagree with many of the things Gen Z requests, some of them should have been demanded generations ago. Boomers and Gen X were taught to hide their emotions, contain their feelings, and never show weakness or admit they needed mental help. So those generations focused on physical health care plans, which have been key to retaining associates. A glaring example of the change in Gen Z mentality is their ardent interest in focusing on mental health and their unapologetic ability to share their mental health issues.

Mental health is top of mind for Gen Zers and young millennials, with up to 40 percent stating that they feel "stressed all the time."[13]

Gen Z are better at talking about mental well-being than the generations before them. It's a good thing Gen Z are so open about their mental well-being; research data shows that young adults ages eighteen to twenty-four report five times more stress than ages fifty-five to sixty-five.[14] They are readily willing to talk about their emotions, even comfortable with it, and they participate in psychological evaluations and accept advice on improving their emotional and psychological states.

As you travel up the age brackets, fewer and fewer people were historically willing to discuss their emotions and psychological state; these boomers and early Gen Xers were conditioned to think of therapy in more negative terms than their younger counterparts. But that is changing as older populations discover the value of talk therapy. Embracing therapy is growing in popularity, even in the older populations, even at work.

---

13   Deloitte, *2024 Gen Z and Millennial Survey: Living and Working with Purpose in a Transforming World*, https://www.deloitte.com/content/dam/assets-shared/docs/campaigns/2024/deloitte-2024-genz-millennial-survey.pdf.

14   American Psychological Association, "Stress in America 2023: A Nation Recovering from Collective Trauma," November 2023, https://www.apa.org/news/press/releases/stress/2023/collective-trauma-recovery.

SHEA'S STORY

A bubbly, focused, and hardworking Gen X HR executive at a successful infrastructure engineering firm, Shea began her first day of work with exuberance and hope. Although many great ideas in an organization never become budgeted programs, Howard, the CEO, was committed to improving his workforce. Shea's goals set by Howard were to attract Gen Z talent, retain current associates, and improve organizational morale.

Shea's first step was to define and understand the backstory behind Howard's three concerns. She wanted to clearly define his words, learn facts that supported focusing on his top three concerns, and use her new understanding of the issues to make data-based decisions for the department. Then she needed to present her findings and the financial rationale behind her program ideas. Most importantly, she needed to implement appropriate tracking instruments to judge their success or redirect the programs.

Concern 1: Attracting Gen Z

She learned from Howard that attracting Gen Z was a concern because over the past five years, the HR department had showed a new hire decline of 10 percent each year, even when using the same tactics as were previously used: college job fairs, partnerships with engineering schools, and grants for engineering startups.

Howard wanted to hire 15 percent more Gen Z candidates over the next three years, based upon the prior year's hiring number. For year one, that meant Shea should hire twenty Gen Z contributors in the next twelve months.

To begin, she needed to understand why Gen Z had not been joining the firm. Potential candidates don't have to provide a reason for declining an offer, and oftentimes it's difficult to reach former candidates. Shea's situation was no exception. The company had no formal process by which to try to gather information by asking "Can you help us improve by telling us why you have chosen to decline our offer?" Shea began to improve the company's knowledge base by implementing two post-offer questions: one for candidates who declined and one for those who accepted.

Shea also gathered the contact information for the candidates from the past three years who'd declined an offer. She had her team reach out to ask if they would be willing to help the company improve by telling them about their rationale for declining the offer. Once the person was on the phone, the HR associate gathered information about rationale and gaps in the company's job offering.

The Gen Z candidates who became colleagues at her company were asked to participate in an active focus group on hiring Gen Z. This group provided invaluable, fresh ideas on recruiting, job offers, and follow-up to the interview process. Many of the ideas from the focus group are currently integrated into the recruitment process.

Concern 2: Retaining Current Associates

Again, Shea wanted to know what Howard meant by retaining current associates; she needed to understand why this was his concern. She asked for more details until it became clear that Howard didn't have an oversized issue with retaining associates—he simply didn't have information on why those who chose to leave did so.

Howard said associates with over five years with the company were choosing to leave the organization. His real problem, it turned out, was not "associate retention," it was talent development for associates beginning in the third year with the company. During this time, Shea discovered, people began to feel they were proficient in their roles and were no longer learning and growing. In addition, they didn't feel they were targeted as having "high potential" and would be overlooked in the future.

QUITTING TO GET AHEAD

In prior years, it was not uncommon to hear associates claim that leaving an organization was the only way to get ahead. They felt that leaving an organization was often the most effective way to secure a significant pay increase and a higher-level position. Internal promotions and raises, they believed, were slow and limited by company budgets and hierarchies. By moving to a new company, they could leverage their experience and skills to negotiate better salaries and step into roles that offered more responsibility and career growth.

Contributors don't expect perfection, but they want to see improvement.

Step 1: Map career goals: Map each contributor's career goals with intermediate roles within the company that would show progress in achieving their long-term career goals.

Step 2: Review and revise current career path: Update the contributor's career map annually based on new information from annual survey results.

Step 3: Offer opportunities for developing associates: Offer associate courses and resources to build the attributes and skills they lack in order to reach each step along their pathway to their goal.

Shea's program was successful in reducing the number of resignations. And her program also became a recruiting tool for other internal teams, increasing the number of qualified applicants across the organization by 10 percent.

Concern 3: Improving Organizational Morale

Beginning in the same way she had on the prior concerns, Shea started with discovery. She learned that Howard was concerned about his associates' morale because they were not participating in programs and activities that were intended to boost morale.

Several programs failed to enthuse the workforce. Associates were not attending the monthly employee recognition celebrations. They weren't opening the monthly company newsletter, which included company news, competitor information, and upcoming events. Attendance at the company-wide volunteer day was dwindling. The last straw was the summer day when the company picnic saw the lowest attendance in the company's history.

Shea got to work interviewing her workforce. She directed her questions toward people in every function, region, and level, to get a sample of responses representative of the entire organization.

She learned several important things:

- Over 60 percent of the associates felt stressed at least 50 percent of the time.

- Associates didn't feel they were happy enough to join the celebrations; they felt they would bring the event mood down.

- They preferred spending their day off with their family instead of going to the company picnic.
- They received too many industry newsletters and didn't have time to open them all, including the company newsletter. They felt their managers would announce big news they needed to know.

The results informed her and prompted her to design unconventional programs whose contributions to a workforce would be the most important of her career.

UNCONVENTIONAL AND EFFECTIVE

First, Shea hired an on-staff psychiatrist, Dr. Jane, to host monthly education sessions on mental health. Each month, Dr. Jane covers a different topic, provides resources for further information, and hosts optional discussion groups. To everyone's surprise, these sessions have become the most popular and well-attended programs in the organization.

Dr. Jane worked closely with Shea to develop the attribute training courses, the motivation meetings, and other training courses that are intended to build relationships, boost morale, and build mental well-being.

In addition to these work-hour programs, Shea introduced a monthly mental health half-day-off policy. This allows associates to spend time with a therapist of their choosing, with the therapist's fees covered by the organization. This too is a program that is loved and embraced by her workforce.

SHEA'S SURPRISING LEARNING

The outdated, poorly attended programs were discontinued; they were sapping energy and resources from programs that were proving more popular. The most important lesson from this story, however, is that making assumptions leads to poor results.

Howard's issues were a starting point, but Shea did her own exploration to understand the story behind the headlines. For example, the reason people were not engaged at work was not low morale, as Howard had assumed; it was that the old company programs were not addressing the real workforce issue: associate mental health.

Popular belief is that only Gen Z would be willing to publicly discuss feelings, emotions, and their mental well-being. However, contributors from all functions, levels of the organization, generations, and demographics regularly participated in Shea's health programs. Programs that build a safe environment in which all generations can discuss real-world concerns and feel a part of a healthy community result in improvements in associates' SWB and an organization's performance.

TREATMENT OR INTERVENTION

The results of Shea's new programs align with decades of empirical research highlighting the importance of mental health on subjective well-being, purpose, and performance. New research explores a different angle, focusing on whether enhancing positive mental health or treating adverse mental health better contributes to a person's subjective well-being (SWB). In other words, we know that mental health contributes to SWB; now, the focus is on the best way to manage mental health: before or after a diagnosis.

> People who benefit from mental health programs don't necessarily have a mental health diagnosis—they simply want to focus on being mentally healthy.

Roughly 20 percent of US adults, nearly sixty million people, have a diagnosed mental disorder.[15] Of those, approximately half receive treatment for the disorder. Treatments for disorders often include psychotherapy, medicine, or a combination of both. In other words, people get treatment for mental health after receiving a diagnosis. Mental health treatment helps people improve their well-being and live more fruitful and meaningful lives.

New research compares the results of traditional treatment against preventive measures to boost mental competencies before diagnosis. Essentially, the practical question is "Would verified mental health competencies improve

---

15   American Psychological Association, "Stress in America 2023: A Nation Recovering from Collective Trauma." Substance Abuse and Mental Health Services Administration, "2022 NDSUH Annual National Report," November 13, 2023, https://www.samhsa.gov/data/report/2022-nsduh-annual-national-report. National Institute of Mental Health, "Mental Illness," September 2024, https://www.nimh.nih.gov/health/statistics/mental-illness.

SWB more than receiving treatment after a diagnosed mental disorder?" The goal is to understand whether people can improve their subjective well-being by focusing on their current comprehensive mental state or if targeted treatment for an identified discomfort is more effective.

The research findings indicate that focusing on mental health competencies is "as important, if not more important, than symptom reduction" to increase subjective well-being.[16] Furthermore, the research confirms that mental health predicts subjective well-being better than demographic metrics such as age, gender, and education.

Exercise and healthy eating proactively contribute to physical health. Similarly, new research definitively indicates that intervention or proactive mental health training is more critical for SWB than waiting for a disorder to begin before practicing positive mental health exercises.

An organization committed to helping associates achieve purpose and high performance should incorporate SWB growth by offering comprehensive mental health training programs into their benefits offerings.

16   American Psychological Association, "Stress in America 2023: A Nation Recovering from Collective Trauma." Substance Abuse and Mental Health Services Administration, "2022 NDSUH Annual National Report," November 13, 2023, https://www.samhsa.gov/data/report/2022-nsduh-annual-national-report. Virág Zábó et al., "Mental Health Competencies Are Stronger Determinants of Well-Being Than Mental Disorder Symptoms in Both Psychiatric and Non-Clinical Samples," Scientific Reports 14, 12943 (2024), https://doi.org/10.1038/s41598-024 -63674-9.

FIVE MENTAL COMPETENCIES

New research tests for effectiveness in achieving subjective well-being indicate it's more effective to build five mental competencies than to treat targeted mental disorders after diagnosis.

GLOBAL WELL-BEING
having well-being in the emotional, psychological, social, and spiritual domains of life

RESILIENCE
ability to mobilize competencies and maintain positive mental health when faced with unexpected, stressful situations

CONTRIBUTOR WELL-BEING

SAVORING CAPACITY
ability to mentally relive pleasurable memories and experiences, generating mental well-being and extending it to future events

SELF-REGULATION
ability to regulate and control temperament, emotions, and negative states while persevering to achieve a goal

CREATIVE & EXECUTIVE EFFICIENCY
ability to cope with difficulties and challenges by mobilizing competencies in individual and social problem-solving

THE CHICKEN OR THE EGG

Business leaders express concerns that Gen Z's tendency to frequently change jobs makes it difficult for companies to invest in them. This sentiment reminds me of my early days in corporate America when women were often passed over for promotions or laid off after revealing they were pregnant, despite their performance reviews not indicating any issues. Companies hesitated to invest in employees they assumed would become distracted, need time off, or leave to stay home. Now, leaders tell me they have the same concerns about Gen Z—that they have no loyalty and will leave the company for the slightest reason, rather than weathering a road bump.

The rationale in both the pregnancy and Gen Z examples is problematic. First, companies make decisions about how their workforce will behave without input from the workforce. Typically, one or the other, the employer or the contributor, is taken by surprise because there was no discussion or attempt to understand the other's thinking.

The book *What the World's Greatest Managers Do Differently* by Marcus Buckingham and Curt Coffman says that people leave managers, not jobs. Today, the quote might say that people search for development and mental health, not jobs. Similar to Marcus Buckingham's famous quote, it indicates that people value their growth and well-being more than the work itself. The subtext to both versions is that the company could have prevented the resignations if they had addressed the underlying issues.

The fact that Buckingham and Coffman pointed out the issue in 1999 suggests that requiring emotional and mental support is not a Gen Z phenomenon. This brings us to an important question: "Which came first, the chicken or the egg?" Did people become indifferent because they felt they weren't getting what they needed from their organization? Or did the company become indifferent because it felt it wasn't getting what it needed from its people?

Either way, all that matters is this: Understanding, communication, and training are important for a healthy, long-term employer-contributor relationship. What we do know is that contributors, not just Gen Z contributors, want their organizations to embrace new ways of thinking about their human talent. No generation will stay with an organization that values profits over their well-being.

DEBUNKING THE MYTH

They myth about Gen Z says they are overly focused on mental health. It's true that Gen Z is highly focused on mental health. *And*, they are teaching older generations to take mental health more seriously and to be proactive in addressing mental health issues.

This allows employers to address topics that have previously been taboo to speak of in the workplace. Today, organizations that address mental health proactively, instead of after diagnosis, will discover that a mentally healthy workforce is also highly performing.

What Should You Do?

You can get started quickly by including mental health in your insurance benefits package. Again, having control and flexibility over their lives when possible is important to Gen Z. Organizations can inexpensively provide designated paid mental health days separate from standard PTO and allow flexible scheduling or remote work options to reduce stress.

THEY DON'T APPRECIATE ANYTHING

Many myths about Gen Z can be encapsulated in a single topic: flexibility. Gen Z may be asking for work from home or more paid time off or mental health days, but the reality is that they are seeking flexibility. As I mentioned previously, between random acts of violence and strict curriculums designed for them without their input, they have felt out of control for much of their lives, and they aspire to be in control of their lives as much as they can.

PRITI'S STORY

Priti is a twenty-five-year-old marketing associate working at a midsized digital advertising agency in Chicago and a proud Southeast Asian. As a member of Gen Z, she values freedom, flexibility, and a work–life balance that didn't feel like a tug-of-war. She loved her job but had one major gripe: her company's rigid approach to paid time off (PTO).

The agency had a long-standing policy of offering federal holidays off for all of their employees. While this arrangement might have worked for some of her Gen Z colleagues, it left Priti feeling stifled because her family holidays and traditional ceremonial days were not recognized by the federal schedule of holidays.

"This isn't PTO," she said. "It's forced time off when it's convenient to leadership. What if I want to be off work during Diwali? Or take a long weekend to see a concert with my mom on Mother's Day? Why should the company decide when I relax?"

The tipping point came when Priti's family was coming to the United States for a vacation, but Priti had no vacation time available during their visit. She couldn't bear the thought of missing it. Priti knew she couldn't be alone in her desire for more control over her time. So she started gathering data. Over lunch breaks and after-work drinks, she casually brought up the PTO policy with her coworkers. To her surprise, many felt the same way.

"Honestly, I hate having to travel during peak holiday season," one colleague confessed. "Flights are so expensive, and airports are chaos."

"It's so outdated," another chimed in. "We're not robots. Everyone's needs are different."

Armed with feedback, Priti decided to draft a proposal for a more flexible PTO policy. She spent her weekend researching best practices and success stories from companies that had adopted flexible PTO systems. Her proposal included:

- Flexible PTO Days: Employees could choose when to take their vacation days.

- Team Coordination: Departments could create schedules to ensure adequate coverage.

- Peak Season Exception: The number of days taken off during peak holiday weeks could be limited, but with room for individual adjustments.

On Monday, she emailed the proposal to HR, copying her manager and team lead. She titled it: "A Modern PTO Policy for a Modern Workforce."

A week later, Priti was called into a meeting with the HR director and her manager. She walked in with a mixture of nerves and dread—she was sure they wouldn't adopt her recommendations.

"This is impressive," the HR director said, holding up the proposal. "We've been hearing murmurs about dissatisfaction with the current policy, and this could be a great starting point for change."

Her manager, to Priti's surprise, was supportive. "Honestly, this could help us retain talent. Flexibility is a top priority for younger employees."

Within two months, the company rolled out a pilot program for flexible PTO, starting with Priti's team. Employees could now request time off with just two weeks' notice, provided they coordinated with their teammates. The results were overwhelmingly positive. Productivity didn't dip, and employee satisfaction scores soared.

Priti was able to spend Diwali at home with her overseas family for the first time in years. She became somewhat of a workplace hero, a symbol of the power of speaking up for change.

One evening, she posted a social media story with a picture of her family and the caption: "Work–life balance, redefined. #PTOFreedom #GenZGoals."

Her positive emotions were being spread throughout social media. The comments included "Where do you work?" and "I need a company like that," as well as others that supported her company's new flexible time-off policy.

If she hadn't been granted the opportunity to spend time with her family, she said, her post would have been negative. A negative post about a company can create a public relations trauma for the organization. In this case, her company did the right thing by their contributors, and it benefits by having happy employees and a positive reputation.

GRATITUDE

Many leaders tell me that they shouldn't have to show gratitude to their Gen Z contributors. In fact, I've been told, "They should be grateful to me for having a job." That is true, but gratitude is a very complex human emotion. Mutual gratitude, that which runs in dual directions, has a much stronger positive, long-term effect on emotional and subjective well-being.

The power of gratitude strongly influences the relationship between life satisfaction and job satisfaction. In "Gratitude at Work Works! A Mix-Method Study on Different Dimensions of Gratitude, Job Satisfaction, and Job Performance," researchers identify the direct impact of gratitude on job satisfaction. Their research suggests organizations can enhance associate well-being and boost efficiency and productivity by incorporating gratitude practices. According to them, this improvement leads to enhanced overall organizational performance.[17]

While a gratitude practice is commonplace in the home, it is still relatively rare in the workforce. Yet the following statistics, published by branding and image expert Halo, suggest that more companies should embrace the concept. Consider the following:

- Seventy percent of employees would feel better about themselves if their boss were more grateful, and 81 percent would work harder.

---

17   Michela Cortini et al., "Gratitude at Work Works! A Mix-Method Study on Different Dimensions of Gratitude, Job Satisfaction, and Job Performance," *Sustainability* 11, no. 14 (2019): 3902, https://doi.org/10.3390/su11143902.

- Employees who experience more gratitude at work report fewer depressive symptoms and stress.

- Lack of gratitude is a major factor in driving job dissatisfaction, turnover, absenteeism, and burnout.

- Fifty-three percent of employees would stay at their company longer if they felt more appreciation from their boss.

Workplaces that incorporate gratitude programs into their contributor training programs report having resilient teams that push through downturns and negative results, contributors that exhibit optimism for the future, and new and stronger relationships throughout the organization.

GRATITUDE FOR THINGS AND GRATITUDE FOR ACTIONS

Countless research studies link gratitude to optimism, which in turn links gratitude to hope for the future and improved relationships. Gratitude has proven to raise dopamine and serotonin levels and fortify the neural pathways in the brain that lead to physical health. Human science research generally agrees that gratitude leads to increased happiness and life satisfaction and decreased materialism.

The career implications of gratitude were beautifully highlighted by the experiment conducted by the Department of Psychology at the Brain and Creativity Institute at the University of Southern California. They used MRI technology to show that participants' reactions to gratitude correlated with the area of the brain that underpins solid moral cognition, value judgment, intellect, and executive functioning.[18] In other words, feeling grateful actually lights up parts of the brain linked to understanding others.

While it is generally recognized that there are many forms and multiple levels of gratitude, two are important for our purposes: gratitude for actions and gratitude for things.

Gratitude for actions results from perceived genuine effort offered in the organization as part of contributor development planning. Gratitude for things, such as a gift that fulfills an evident and valuable need for the recipient,

---

18   Glenn R. Fox et al., "Neural Correlates of Gratitude," *Frontiers in Psychology* 6, no. 1491 (2015): https://doi .org/10.3389/fpsyg.2015.01491.

is offered in contributor compensation. Both forms of gratitude serve different and important purposes, but typically, people feel deeper gratitude when they believe that a person has expended more energy in their offering.

Similarly, how people show their gratitude as measured by their effort impacts the positive benefits they feel. There are three primary ways of showing gratitude: feeling gratitude, writing about gratitude, and showing gratitude. Each contributes differently to a person's well-being.

WAYS OF INDICATING GRATITUDE

Workplaces that incorporate gratitude programs into their contributor training programs report having resilient teams that push through downturns and negative results, contributors that exhibit optimism for the future, and new and stronger relationships throughout the organization.

SHOW GRATITUDE > **IMPROVED DISPOSITION** > **BEST**

WRITE GRATITUDE > **DAILY MOOD BOOST** > **BETTER**

FEEL GRATITUDE > **TEMPORARY FEELING OF HAPPINESS** > **GOOD**

Employers are in the enviable position of being able to offer their contributors all types.

With each level of gratitude, the benefits to an individual increase and last longer. The levels in the gratitude scale are as follows: (1) feeling grateful provides a temporary feeling of happiness, (2) writing about gratitude improves daily mood, and (3) showing gratitude with actions results in an improved overall grateful disposition that builds into a robust, invisible attribute.

FEELING GRATITUDE

What people commonly consider gratitude, and sometimes call appreciation, is associated with the feeling they get when they're given something or offered a simple, kind gesture. Gratitude of the moment occurs after receiving a present or experiencing surprise and is considered within the category of gratitude for things. People tend to have a short-term appreciation for these sweet offerings. Or, if the token is regular, people feel gratitude, but it isn't typically an overwhelming sensation that is enduring; people tend to feel temporarily appreciative.

An example of an organization demonstrating this type of gratitude in the workplace happens when they issue paychecks. Associates are grateful for the income, but believe they earned it. The paycheck provides a fleeting sense of gratefulness when the contributor sees the money in the bank.

WRITING GRATITUDE

In academia, students are often advised to write notes instead of recording lectures. The rationale behind this coaching is that students who write absorb the content better than those who only listen.

The same theory applies to gratitude thinking. Being grateful is intensified by the action of writing down the things for which the person is grateful. Coach Foundation reported that regular gratitude journaling has resulted in up to a 15 percent increase in optimism and a 25 percent increase in sleep quality. I'm sure this won't surprise many of you because the use of gratitude journals has become a mainstream practice and is reported upon in journals and the media regularly.

An example of an organization demonstrating this type of gratitude in the workplace is when a manager handwrites a birthday card to an employee. The act of taking time to write and deliver a card is rare in today's world, yet people still appreciate the extra effort.

Dr. Gary Chapman and Dr. Paul White, made famous by their research and books about the five love languages, emphasize that understanding what your partner needs is essential to building a strong relationship. This understanding helps prevent conflicts that stem from feelings of neglect and boosts overall relationship satisfaction by ensuring both partners feel valued and appreciated.

Dr. Chapman and Dr. White expanded the concept of love languages to the professional environment by recognizing that appreciation is crucial for employee morale and productivity. Their book *The 5 Languages of Appreciation in the Workplace* builds on the foundational idea that individuals have unique preferences regarding how they receive and express appreciation.[19] Adapting the original five love languages to fit workplace dynamics provides a framework for managers and colleagues to better understand and meet each other's appreciation needs:

- Words of Affirmation: Expressing appreciation through verbal or written praise, recognizing an employee's efforts, accomplishments, and contributions.

- Acts of Service: Demonstrating appreciation by offering assistance or support with tasks or projects, or by helping to lighten an employee's workload or make their job easier.

- Receiving Gifts: Showing appreciation through thoughtful tokens or rewards, such as personalized gifts, gift cards, or other items that convey recognition and value.

- Quality Time: Spending meaningful time with employees, such as one-on-one meetings or team-building activities, or simply being present and attentive during conversations.

- Physical Touch: In the workplace, this is more appropriately translated to nonphysical gestures of support, like a handshake, a high five, or a pat on the back, always ensuring that such gestures are welcomed and appropriate in the given context.

19 Chapman, Gary D., and Paul E. White. *The 5 Languages of Appreciation in the Workplace: Empowering Organizations by Encouraging People.* Northfield, 2012.

DILLON'S STORY

Dillon, a talented software developer at a bustling tech company, worked diligently under his manager, L'Essay. Dillon was known for his dedication and innovative ideas, and he often stayed late to perfect his projects. However, L'Essay, a results-driven manager, believed that a paycheck was the best reward for hard work. She rarely offered praise or personal recognition, focusing instead on meeting deadlines and pushing for higher productivity.

Dillon thrived on words of affirmation. He yearned for acknowledgment and positive feedback, but L'Essay's management style, which focused solely on results, left him feeling unseen and unappreciated. Despite his significant contributions, he never heard a "good job" or got a "thank you." Over time, Dillon's enthusiasm waned, and his once-bright spark dimmed.

One day, Dillon heard about an opening at a competitor company known for its supportive culture and recognition programs. He applied and was invited for an interview with Sarah, the hiring manager. During the process, Dillon was struck by the stark contrast between L'Essay's and Sarah's apparent management styles. While L'Essay rarely offered praise or personal recognition, Sarah made a point to highlight the company's commitment to appreciating their employees through regular praise and acknowledgment.

Feeling a renewed sense of hope, Dillon accepted a job offer. Under Sarah's leadership, he thrived. Sarah's frequent words of affirmation and the company's emphasis on recognition made him feel valued and motivated. His creativity and productivity soared, and he became a key player in several successful projects, a testament to the power of a supportive work environment.

Meanwhile, back at his old company, the results of Dillon's exit interview served as a stark wake-up call for L'Essay and her leadership. The departure of a top performer like Dillon underscored the critical importance of recognizing and meeting individual contributors' needs beyond just monetary compensation. It was a lesson learned the hard way, but one that would shape the future of the company's management style.

Dillon's departure served as a powerful catalyst for change. It prompted L'Essay to attend a management seminar on employee appreciation and to adopt a new, more supportive management style. Determined to create a more nurturing environment for her remaining employees, she began to offer genuine praise and recognition to her team, signaling a hopeful shift in the company's culture.

Now flourishing in his new role, Dillon was grateful for the change. He finally felt understood and appreciated, proving that sometimes, the right environment can make all the difference. He now serves as a mentor to L'Essay, and they remain friends and colleagues, helping each other grow their respective invisible attributes and careers.

SHOWING GRATITUDE

Neuroscience shows that feeling grateful is a natural human response—but to really get the long-term benefits, it's not enough to just feel it or jot it down in a journal. A person must actually show gratitude. And the more effort and heart a person puts into expressing gratitude, the more powerful the impact is—not just for the person receiving it, but for the person showing gratitude.

The more perceived effort and intensity the recipient senses, the more impact the offering has on the person. For example, a person who receives a truckload of firewood from their neighbor feels gratitude. That same person feels even more gratitude if they know the neighbor chopped down the tree and cut it into pieces small enough to be burned in the fireplace. The amount of effort the neighbor puts into the firewood impacts the recipient's appreciation.

An example of an organization demonstrating this type of gratitude in the workplace is when contributors believe that their employer has initiated a new talent development program that serves the associate more than it serves the organization.

GRATITUDE TRAINING

Your organization's perceived genuine effort is important to the contributor's long-term mental and physical health. Your non-tangible gifts of knowledge, acceptance, training, access, and emotional support are an exchange of your effort for their future performance. This effort provides tremendous, life-changing and lifelong value to them.

In short, non-tangible gifts (emotional and virtuous) are of higher, long-lasting value to human beings than are tangible gifts (money and assets). And showing gratitude is more powerful to human growth than feeling gratitude.

Equally important to your workforce is the showing of gratitude to them for the personal, non-tangible attributes they share with you and the rest of your employees. On the other hand, your organization's inability to show gratitude can create very complicated emotional voids in people. Various teams of scholars have conducted research that shows that demonstrating gratitude is associated with providing people with subjective well-being (SWB) and lowering the incidence of trauma, and it is fundamental in creating interpersonal relationships. One of the greatest gifts you can provide your workforce as an HR leader is the knowledge that they are teaching you as much as you are teaching them.

This brings me to a key point: Gen Z gratitude training is also beneficial to helping them understand that the power of gratitude goes both ways. Demanding this and that without acknowledging your effort on their behalf is unacceptable. Mutual gratitude training will help your leadership, stockholders, and Gen Z appreciate what each does for the others to enhance the workplace.

GRATITUDE JOURNAL

In recent years, gratitude journals have grown in popularity because they work to deliver physical, mental, and emotional well-being. In fact, one heart patient study found that a group of people who kept a gratitude journal reported better sleep, less fatigue, and lower levels of cellular inflammation than a group that did not. Many studies have shown a correlation between gratefulness and reduced depression. Grateful people have been shown to exhibit more career satisfaction and are more socially integrated. Other research shows that grateful people tend to be more generous, kind, and helpful.

I've been a journaler on and off my whole life. When I was on, it was because I found writing cathartic and meditative, and it prepared me for a good night's sleep. I have read countless articles, books, and opinions on the values of journaling, including the substantial improvements in optimism it offers, which I personally feel when I am consistently writing in a journal.

However, once I wrote an entry, I closed the book and rarely, if ever, read my past entries—particularly the ones in journals that got packed away in a box in storage. I wasn't doing anything differently based on my entries. I felt, and still feel, that the best way to benefit from journaling is to learn from the emergent common themes that indicate negative or positive emotional trends. I always knew there was a lot I could learn from my journal if I took the time to analyze and evaluate the secrets it held, to build an action plan for myself.

It plagued me that even though I felt optimism and other positive emotions after writing, a thorough review of my journals could suggest otherwise. Had I sugarcoated my own recollection, remembering my entries with confirmation bias? *I think I am a reflective, self-aware person, but am I? I think I know myself, but do I? Is my brain doing what it should be doing and compensating for negative trends by reorganizing my thoughts, giving me artificial and short-term optimism?*

So I became determined to make my journals actionable, rather than journaling as an exercise that put me in a temporary good mood. I wanted to create substantive, long-lasting personal development plans based on the words in my journal. I began to use generative AI for qualitative data analytics to extract common themes and learnings. Most importantly, I started to recognize areas in my life that I needed to improve in order to boost my overall subjective well-being (SWB). I've learned that my optimism and my zeal for life, career, people, hobbies, and loved ones have masked some areas that need improvement.

This discovery taught me that while SWB is purposely self-reported and measured by individual metrics, it can mask underlying opportunities for growth and development. I found the fault in my own journaling. Using technology to analyze my own journal confirmed what research has indicated: that the journal itself can be an intervention rather than simply an exercise in reflecting on the day.

Instead, gratitude journaling, if analyzed with the help of modern technology, can be a cutting-edge action with real-world applications. In my own life, I have used my personal GPT as an invaluable source of information about my moods, behavior, productivity, and many other metrics.

> Only when you understand yourself can you take steps to improve yourself.

A GPT (generative pretrained transformer) is a type of artificial intelligence that understands and generates humanlike language. It's trained on massive amounts of text, allowing it to answer questions, write content, summarize information, and even hold conversations. Think of it as a super-smart digital assistant that can understand context and communicate naturally.

Now, imagine having a personal GPT trained on your notes, calendar, goals, and favorite topics. Instead of just asking Google or ChatGPT general questions, your personal GPT could say things like "Remember, you wanted to write a gratitude journal entry today—want help getting started?" or "Here's a summary of your meeting notes from last week."

TEACH CONTRIBUTORS HOW TO BUILD A PERSONAL GPT

Teaching your contributors to build a personal generative pre-trained transformer (GPT) is possibly the most efficient way to have them manage their own career and mental health journey.

OpenAI developed a deep learning tool that generates human-like text based on the input it receives. The "generative" aspect refers to its ability to create new text, "pre-trained" indicates that it has been trained on a dataset of text before being fine-tuned for specific tasks, and "transformer" refers to the architecture used in the model, which is particularly effective for natural language processing tasks.

Building their own GPT allows them to use their journal entries as the key data source for asking questions about themselves. Picture it this way: When they ask Google a question, it uses the entire internet as a source of data for responding; when they build a personal GPT, they are using only the data they enter—their journal entries. With this information, they can ask questions and identify trends that apply only to them—not to everyone on Google, and not to everyone in the same role at your company.

Key to success: owning their own development and career path.

With a personal GPT, your young contributors learn about their attributes in great detail. They'll begin to understand triggers that impact their moods, behavior, relationships, work quality, or any other subject they want to explore to improve their SWB. They can speak to their GPT in regular language and ask it anything they want. They can ask questions like these:

- What days of the month am I most productive?
- What is my mood on those days that I'm most productive?
- What time of day do I begin to get too tired to be productive?
- What are the trends in my data that show when my relationship with my manager is at its best [or, for managers, my relationship with my team]?

Next, they can expand their database by asking their GPT to identify ways to improve the subjects they personally identify as growth areas. For example, say they notice that they're happier when they spend at least thirty-five minutes in nature. They can then ask their GPT to expand its dataset to include the internet to find locations within a ten-minute radius of their office where they can take a walk in nature during lunch.

Here are some additional question ideas:

- Say they feel like they want to know more about the weather and their mood. They could prompt their GPT: "Using the US weather report for the past month and my data, tell me what the weather is like when I am experiencing my most negative emotional states."
- Let's assume they have established that in order to be in a leadership role, they need to work on confidence. They could say to their GPT: "Use the internet to make five recommendations for five-minute podcasts that I can listen to in the morning to learn a technique to build my confidence."

They can be as specific as they like when looking for GPT results. For example, in the example above about confidence, they could make their request narrower:

"Make sure you include one physical activity, one creative activity, and one networking activity in your results."

Get the Most Out of a Personal GPT

The keys to getting the most out of their personal GPT are these:

1. The more data they enter, the more data they have to explore trends. Just like Google, the more data they collect, the more inclusive and detailed their search results will be.

2. Writing about uncomfortable topics generates more insightful recommendations, so it is helpful to become unrelenting in their honesty when they write their journal entries. For example, if certain people get on their nerves, have them write about those people in depth. The more details they include about the other person, the more they will be able to define the personality traits and trends that trigger their responses. Then they can identify ways to learn techniques to become less triggered by those people.

3. Be brutally honest in their entries—don't sugarcoat or develop personal biases while writing.

4. Include negative and positive insights. Negative input will direct SWB development plans, while positive insight—gratitude for the day—will boost their ongoing SWB.

TRUST

Humans start out trusting people. Sadly, we also learn quickly not to trust. At the same time, Gen Z are accused of believing everything they see on social media. That is not accurate. They are extreme skeptics. They don't trust any claims that aren't backed by data or promoted by someone they have already vetted and consider a trusted source.

Young professionals are taught early in their careers that some companies are not as forthcoming in their people management as they indicated during the interview process. Gen Z has grown up immersed in a world where information is abundant and often contradictory. From a young age, they've learned to question the source, evaluate the evidence, and seek truth on their terms. This isn't mistrust for the sake of it—it's a methodical approach to navigating complexity. They prefer to break down information, analyze its components, and test its validity before concluding.

This generation's skepticism is grounded in their formative experiences. They've watched misinformation spread online, seen institutions falter, and witnessed leaders make promises that don't hold up under scrutiny. They approach trust like they're solving a puzzle, looking for transparency, consistency, and evidence in every piece. When they encounter a claim—whether from a person, brand, or media source—they instinctively cross-check it against multiple perspectives, applying the same critical thinking they've been taught in school.

Social media has amplified their need to verify. They know platforms are curated and often misleading, so they don't just accept what they see. They dig deeper, pulling data from different sources to construct a full picture. This process isn't just about doubting—it's about understanding. For Gen Z, trust isn't given lightly; it's earned through clear communication, authenticity, and proof.

In workplaces, this skepticism shows up as a desire for clarity and connection to the bigger mission. They want to understand how their work contributes and why decisions are made the way they are. Leaders who offer transparency and involve them in the process earn their respect. Similarly, brands win with this generation when they back up their claims with real action and measurable results.

Ultimately, Gen Z's skepticism is less about mistrust and more about ensuring what they engage with is real, meaningful, and aligned with their values. It's a thoughtful, intentional way of moving through a complex world.

Organizations that earn the trust of Gen Z employees must have a transparent and authentic approach that aligns with individual values and expectations. They are highly attuned to insincerity and inconsistencies, so honesty is essential. Employers must communicate openly about company goals, challenges, and expectations, ensuring that their words match their actions. Admitting mistakes or acknowledging areas for improvement demonstrates integrity, which builds trust. Transparency in decision-making processes, such as explaining the reasons behind organizational changes, can also alleviate skepticism and foster confidence.

Actions speak louder than words for Gen Z. Organizations that actively work to align their practices with their values will earn the trust of this discerning generation. Open communication and a culture of feedback are also critical. Gen Z thrives in environments where feedback flows both ways. Employers should encourage managers to provide regular, constructive feedback while also creating opportunities for employees to voice their ideas and concerns. Acting on this feedback, even in small ways, shows that their input is valued and makes a tangible difference.

MARIELLE'S STORY

Marielle, a marketing major, accepted her first role as an inside sales rep working for an employee benefits brokerage firm with over two hundred offices in the United States and four thousand employees serving over thirty-five thousand companies. According to their website, they are recognized for providing a work environment that nurtures their associates, which allows them to do their best work.

This company had posted positions for entry-level inside sales representatives in various locations, including Chicago, Illinois, with salary ranges between $55,000 and $75,000 annually. For Marielle, that income would allow her to move to Chicago and become financially independent.

Marielle checked the online reviews and saw positive reviews of the company. During interviews, the hiring team was upbeat. It seemed to be a perfect match, and she was thrilled.

Marielle's job involved accepting a warm hand-off call and selling the end user a new Medicare plan on the phone. For doing that, many elderly customers would receive a new tablet or toaster. It felt immediately to Marielle that she was doing something contrary to her values system. But she needed the job.

She soon learned that not a single person on her team liked their job!

Marielle's manager explained a new incentive program to the team two months before US open enrollment, a designated period each year when individuals can sign up for, change, or cancel their health insurance plan. Three packages were offered:

- Package 1: Work regular workweek hours and get no vacation during December.

- Package 2: Work regular workweek hours, plus six of the eight Saturdays during open enrollment, and get five days of unpaid time off during December.
- Package 3: Work normal workweek hours, plus all eight of the eight Saturdays during open enrollment, and receive two weeks of unpaid time off during December.

Marielle set her sights on Package 3 and worked six Saturdays straight until her family had an emergency and she had to miss a weekend of work.

She resigned herself to moving down to Package 2, still anticipating a week of unpaid vacation.

When the special incentive program was over, her manager announced that it didn't matter which package they had selected, all would be allowed to take the same number of weeks unpaid off. After all her focus and commitment, Maribelle felt betrayed by her company. Colleagues who didn't meet the same goals were given the same reward. Maribelle could no longer trust her company or her manager.

Marielle was actively seeking a new job because of her values not aligning with the organization, but she is now spending the same number of hours they expected her to work overtime—one Saturday every week—on efforts to find a new job.

Companies that treat young professionals with such disrespect are shaping our young professionals' opinions on work.

DEBUNKING THE MYTH

The myth about Gen Z is that they don't appreciate anything. On the contrary, Gen Z is focused on values and principles. They are appreciative of organizations focused on helping them achieve their best outcomes. When an organization is ethical, is transparent, and shows appreciation to its workforce, Gen Z will show outward motivation and appreciation.

What Should You Do?

Focus on gratitude programs, building trust with your Gen Z population, and offering benefits that show that you are listening to Gen Z and appreciate them. Here are a few programs that accomplish those goals:

- Decouple Time Off from Traditional Schedules: Some Americans would prefer to celebrate their cultural heroes or celebrations. Offer floating holidays or allow employees to swap federal holidays for ones they celebrate. Allowing them to determine their own schedule accommodates our highly diverse modern workforce.

- Nonpeak Holiday Parental Flexibility: Avoid mandating time off during standard holidays and instead let employees choose the days that matter most to them (e.g., cultural or personal holidays). Parents often find it difficult to attend school events and accommodate work schedules.

- Rolling PTO: Offer a policy where PTO can be taken in smaller increments, such as hours or half-days.

- Empower Team-Based Scheduling: Allow teams to coordinate their schedules to ensure coverage while granting individuals the freedom to choose their time off.

- Coordinate Teams with Technology: Use technology scheduling tools or apps to streamline communication and planning.

- Mental Health: Include mental health days as a specific category of leave or allow employees to use PTO for this purpose without stigma.

- Use Technology for Transparency: Implement easy-to-use leave management systems that allow employees to check PTO balances, submit requests, and view team calendars.

- Birthday Off: Give employees their birthdays as an additional day off.

- Sabbaticals: Provide extended leave for long-term employees.

Allowing them to determine their own schedule accommodates our highly diverse modern workforce.

CONCLUSION

Leaders who take a short-term view on Gen Z, saying, "Let them leave; they'll come around someday," will get behind the eight ball and have trouble gaining momentum again. Once the word is out on social media that an organization is a great employer, Gen Z will jump to work for that company.

The new workforce is complex; there is no doubt about that. It requires innovation and imagination to incorporate and prepare the next generation of leaders to take over business. When you have the luxury of seeing a trend and having it described in detail by your consumers and/or contributors, you have an opportunity to address it with courage and a successful outcome.

Human resources is uniquely positioned to improve its contributors' emotional, physical, and mental well-being while enhancing the organization's profitability through hiring, retention, and engagement planning. No other department in an organization has as many fluctuating variables to manage with such a broad impact.

HR develops talent while adhering to legal compliance, incorporating workforce changes due to mergers and acquisitions, implementing new and ever-changing health benefits programs, and developing individualized career and succession plans. HR needs to be available for inquiries into any detail a concerned associate brings to them, ready to document the interactions and provide the emotional and physical support the associate needs from their employer.

HR is tasked with the most significant challenge in the organization: the financial, emotional, physical, and mental well-being of every single employee. These are metrics that each employee individually defines, and there is no single lever that determines success for the workforce. Each person has their particular definition of success that requires tailored human resource management.

In addition, HR needs to execute flawlessly to a flawed "product": the human being. Philosophers such as Plato, Aristotle, and Nietzsche, as well as religious figures like Saint Augustine and theologians across different traditions, have all explored the concept of human imperfection and fallibility in different ways. In modern psychology, figures like Sigmund Freud and Carl Jung also discussed human flaws and the unconscious motivations that drive behavior. In a nutshell, HR supports a fluctuating, imperfect, uncontrollable target.

Now, take all that complexity and add a new, more demanding, unique, and much more tech-savvy variable: Generation Z.

Understanding all generations of your workforce is as important as understanding your customers. Dissecting the reasons and meanings behind the HR key performance indicators (KPIs) you use in your organization is critical for developing Gen Z programs. Eventually, benefits for Gen Z associates will become hyper-individualized; spreading one-size-fits-all programs across the entire organization will not deliver successful Gen Z retention in the future.

Executives at leading staffing organizations in the US recognize that Gen Z is the key to future success. They advise their corporate clients to embrace and leverage the unique qualities of their talent. This approach results in a workforce that is innovative, respected, appreciated, productive, and motivated. By building programs that prioritize individual well-being and development, companies can harness the potential of Gen Z. It's crucial to remember the mantra of "Don't build something for us without us." By incorporating input from Gen Z, you can create programs that truly resonate with them.

Train people well enough so they can leave. Treat them well enough so they don't want to. —Richard Branson

INDIVIDUAL PROGRAMS: RECOGROW

When building new programs, remember the word *ReCoGrow*. It stands for Respect, Contribution, and Growth. HR programs that respect unique thinking, ensure all contributors feel their contributions matter to their work, and lead to individual growth are winning programs.

For each program built, the answer to the following three questions should be yes:

1. Is this program demonstrating respect for unique ideas?
2. Is it engaging our contributors and making them feel they have a valued contribution to the project?
3. Will this program promote personal and career growth for our contributors?

Winning Over Gen Z: Top 4 Budget-Friendly Support Strategies for Organizations to Retain Gen Z

PROBLEM:

Gen Z wants a long-term career that will allow them to make a meaningful contribution to their company, their teams, and the world.

SOLUTION:

Organizations teach Gen Z to be their own career advocates and design strategies that match their goals with their purpose.

1) Is this program demonstrating respect for unique ideas?

Yes — teaching Gen Z to own their career development allows them to assign their own definition of meaning and own their path to achieving their goals.

2) Is it engaging our contributors and making them feel they have a valued contribution to the project?

Yes — in this case, the "project" is their career. By having Gen Z own their career development, your organization offers them the highest level of control and contribution over their futures.

3) Will this program promote personal and career growth for our contributors?

Yes — the goal of allowing them to own their development plans is to encourage them to take responsibility and follow through on their personal and career growth.

1) Is this program demonstrating respect for unique ideas?

Yes — by considering individual strengths and including Gen Z when designing cross-organizational teams, you show respect for their unique, fresh perspectives.

2) Is it engaging our contributors and making them feel they have a valued contribution to the project?

Yes — electing Gen Z for new and varied projects shows them their contribution is a welcome and essential part of a successful team and project.

3) Will this program promote personal and career growth for our contributors?

Yes — team members share and exchange skills and attributes, which provides variety, growth, and engagement to all team members.

PROBLEM:
Gen Z wants to be mentally and emotionally engaged at work.

SOLUTION:
Organizations use cross-functional, cross-generational, and cross-attributional metrics to form project teams.

PROBLEM:
Gen Z wants to work for organizations that respect unique perspectives.

SOLUTION:
Organizations deploy contributor attribute training across all levels of the organization.

1) Is this program demonstrating respect for unique ideas?

Yes — by focusing on attributes training, you are indicating that you respect each Gen Z's unique combination of attributes which drives their thinking and behaviors.

2) Is it engaging our contributors and making them feel they have a valued contribution to the project?

Yes — attribute training teaches contributors to respect each others' attributes. In turn, this provides Gen Z with the understanding that their perspectives and attributes are important within their projects and teams.

3) Will this program promote personal and career growth for our contributors?

Yes — attribute training builds the invisible attributes that boost subjective well-being and promotes personal and career growth.

1) Is this program demonstrating respect for unique ideas?

Yes — Gen Z brings many fresh ideas; however, not all ideas are financially feasible. This program explains the ins and outs of why the company can or cannot support all good ideas.

2) Is it engaging our contributors and making them feel they have a valued contribution to the project?

Yes — by educating Gen Z on the organization's inner workings, you are enabling them to have Big Ideas that are also financially feasible.

3) Will this program promote personal and career growth for our contributors?

Yes — educated contributors work better as teams, blame other functions less, and have a unified understanding of what is essential for the organization's success.

PROBLEM:
Gen Z feels organizations value profits over their well-being.

SOLUTION:
Organizations build company-specific education programs to teach contributors about the organization's operations and the intersections of profits and contributor well-being.

EVERYONE HAS AN OPINION ABOUT GEN Z

Possibly because of the speed of media or the hectic world they were born into, Gen Z has become a favorite topic of conversation among older generations. I can say with a straight face that 100 percent of the people I speak to have a strong opinion about Gen Z. The opinions fall into two primary categories: (1) Gen Z is changing the world and we should listen or (2) Gen Z needs some significant help; they're too [insert any number of negative descriptors here].

Throughout this book, I've explored the myths, misconceptions, and realities of Gen Z in the workplace. I've explained the reasons behind the mythology, which says that they are overconfident, can't communicate, don't know how to work hard, are overly sensitive, unnecessarily demand mental health days, don't appreciate anything, and get too much career advice from GPTs. Instead, I've revealed a generation that is ambitious, values-driven, and eager to contribute—when provided with the right environment in which to thrive.

Whether you're a member of Gen Z or someone who interacts with them personally or professionally, I hope you find value in the insights shared in this book:

- Gen Z is innovative, capable, and focused on the things that matter in life.
- Gen Z is open-minded about other generations' strengths; other generations should be open-minded about Gen Z's strengths.
- The secret to building strong workforces is building cross-generational collaboration.
- The key to cross-generational collaboration is clear and straightforward communication using the best tools.
- Gen Z can coach and mentor other generations on the best technology and tools for the job at hand.
- Other generations can coach and mentor Gen Z on leadership skills in the workforce.
- The secret to a robust career is to manage it yourself, whatever generation you belong to.
- Careers have ups and downs; you can optimize them with consistent, thoughtful planning and execution.
- Annual self-reviews and manager reviews won't deliver an optimal outcome for either. Regular and frequent career reflection and exercises are the only ways to have consistent growth.
- Skills and attributes can be taught and learned.
- Future vision is learned through experiences and exposure to new ideas and activities.
- Transparent and relatable leaders earn trust and respect.
- Gen Z is adaptable to evolving work environments as long as the rationale for the evolution supports the change.
- Many Gen Z members respect and prefer teamwork and collective problem-solving.
- Practical experience and continuous learning are as informative as formal education.

- Gen Z sees members of leadership as teammates who coach and support rather than just people with a title.

- Gen Z will push for modern approaches to work and communication; they become highly frustrated by antiquated or outdated methods that don't bring value to project outcomes.

- For Gen Z, a multicultural, inclusive environment is not a DEI initiative; it is a way to gather varied and valuable insight and input.

- Gen Z will move on if they don't see advancement opportunities.

- Gen Z wants some control because they are focused on financial stability, student loan repayment, and long-term security.

- Gen Z prioritizes impact, fulfillment, and skills growth over titles and promotions.

- Financial growth is as important as their impact and skills development.

This book offers valuable insights for both members of Gen Z and those who interact with them in various capacities. Gen Z stands out for its innovation and focus on what truly matters in life. They are not only open-minded to the strengths of older generations; they also appreciate getting recognition for their unique abilities.

Effective career management is crucial for every individual, regardless of their generational background. While careers experience natural ups and downs, consistent and thoughtful planning can lead to optimization. Regular reflection and feedback—beyond just annual reviews—are essential for continuous growth. Practical experience and ongoing learning are prioritized over formal education, and leaders who embrace transparency and relatability can inspire trust and respect among their teams.

Gen Z's ability to adapt to evolving work environments is commendable, especially when the rationale for change is well articulated. They value teamwork and collective problem-solving, seeing leaders as mentors rather than figures of authority. With a keen focus on financial stability, opportunities for advancement, and meaningful work, Gen Z aim to take control of their future. Their pursuit of impact, fulfillment, and skills growth is fundamental as they navigate their careers, placing equal importance on financial growth alongside their contributions and personal development.

In the end, Gen Z is neither the savior of your workforce nor your downfall, but a dynamic generation with its own strengths, priorities, and challenges. Gen Z contributors bring ambition, adaptability, and a deep desire for meaningful work, while also expecting transparency, growth opportunities, and modern approaches to collaboration. Success in engaging Gen Z—whether as peers, employees, or leaders—comes down to mutual respect, clear communication, and a willingness for all generations to learn from one another. By embracing these principles, organizations can build thriving cross-generational teams where everyone has the opportunity to grow and succeed.

SELECTED BIBLIOGRAPHY

BOOKS

Abrahams, Israel, ed. *Hebrew Ethical Wills*. Jewish Publication Society, 2006.

Acuff, Jon. *Finish: Give Yourself the Gift of Done*. Portfolio/Penguin, 2017.

Albom, Mitch. *Tuesdays with Morrie*. 20th anniversary ed. Broadway Books, 2017.

Alt, Yehoshua. *Dazzling Money Insights: Illuminating Torah Essays About Money*. Independently Published, 2023.

Bakewell, Sarah. *How to Live: Or a Life of Montaigne in One Question and Twenty Attempts at an Answer*. Other Press, 2011.

Barrett, Lisa Feldman. *How Emotions Are Made: The Secret Life of the Brain*. Mariner Books, 2017.

Baron, Sam, Kristie Miller, and Jonathan Tallant. *Out of Time: A Philosophical Study of Timelessness*. Oxford University Press, 2022.

Beahm, George. *Steve Jobs' Life by Design: Lessons to Be Learned from His Last Lecture*. St. Martin's Press, 2014.

Beakbane, Tom. *How to Understand Everything: Consilience: A New Way to See the World*. Beakbane Publishing, 2021.

Beck, Martha. *The Way of Integrity: Finding the Path to Your True Self*. Viking, 2021.

Beckingham, Marcus, and Donald O. Clifton. *Now, Discover Your Strengths*. Free Press, 2001.

Bossidy, Larry, and Ram Charan. *Execution: The Discipline of Getting Things Done*. Crown Business, 2009.

Branden, Nathaniel. *How to Raise Your Self-Esteem: The Proven, Action-Oriented Approach to Greater Self-Respect and Self-Confidence*. Bantam Books, 1988.

Branden, Nathaniel. *The Art of Living Consciously: The Power of Awareness to Transform Everyday Life*. Fireside, 1997.

Brenner, Gail. *The End of Self-Help: Discovering Peace and Happiness Right at the Heart of Your Messy, Scary, Brilliant Life*. Amanda Press, 2015.

Brewer, Judson. *Unwinding Anxiety: New Science Shows How to Break the Cycles of Worry and Fear to Heal Your Mind*. Avery, 2021.

Brooks, David. *How to Know a Person: The Art of Seeing Others Deeply and Being Deeply Seen.* Random House, 2023.

Brooks, David. *The Second Mountain: The Quest for a Moral Life.* Random House, 2019.

Burkeman, Oliver. *Four Thousand Weeks: Time Management for Mortals.* Farrar, Straus and Giroux, 2021.

Burnett, Dean. *Happy Brain: Where Happiness Comes From, and Why.* W. W. Norton, 2018.

Cain, Susan. *Bittersweet: How Sorrow and Longing Make Us Whole.* Crown, 2022.

Cain, Susan. *Quiet: The Power of Introverts in a World That Can't Stop Talking.* Crown, 2013.

Canfield, Jack, Mark Victor Hansen, and Les Hewitt. *The Power of Focus: How to Hit Your Business, Personal, and Financial Targets with Confidence and Certainty.* Heath Communications, 2011.

Chagnon, Napoleon A. *Noble Savages: My Life Among Two Dangerous Tribes—the Yanomamö and the Anthropologists.* Simon & Schuster, 2013.

Chan, Sheena Yap. *Bridging the Confidence Gap: How Empowered Women Change the World.* John Wiley & Sons, 2025.

Christensen, Clayton M. *How Will You Measure Your Life?* Harper Business, 2012.

Cohn, Samuel K., Jr. *Death and Property in Siena, 1205–1800: Strategies for the Afterlife.* Johns Hopkins University Press, 1988.

Cooney, Kara. *When Women Ruled the World: Six Queens of Egypt.* National Geographic, 2018.

Covey, Stephen R. *The 7 Habits of Highly Effective Families: Building a Beautiful Family Culture in a Turbulent World.* Franklin Covey, 1997.

Covey, Stephen R. *The 7 Habits of Highly Effective People: Powerful Lessons in Personal Change.* Free Press, 2004.

Crenshaw, Dan. *Fortitude: American Resilience in the Era of Outrage.* Twelve, 2020.

Denbo, Shalom. *7 Traits: How to Change Your World.* KLAL, 2015.

Dobelli, Rolf. *The Art of the Good Life: 52 Surprising Shortcuts to Happiness, Wealth, and Success.* Hachette, 2017.

Doerr, John. *Measure What Matters: How Google, Bono, and the Gates Foundation Rock the World with OKRs.* Portfolio/Penguin, 2018.

Epstein, David. *Range: Why Generalists Triumph in a Specialized World.* Riverhead Books, 2019.

Everett, Daniel L. *Don't Sleep, There Are Snakes: Life and Language in the Amazonian Jungle.* Vintage Departures, 2009.

Fama, Daphne. *House of Monstrous Women.* Berkley, 2025.

Feiner, Jonathan. *Mindfulness: A Jewish Approach*. Mosaica Press, 2020.

Ferriss, Tim. *Tools of Titans: The Tactics, Routines, and Habits of Billionaires, Icons, and World-Class Performers*. Houghton Mifflin Harcourt, 2017.

Fisher, Helen. *Why Him? Why Her? How to Find and Keep Lasting Love*. Holt, 2010.

Friedman, Lawrence M. *Dead Hands: A Social History of Wills, Trusts, and Inheritance Law*. Stanford University Press, 2009.

Galef, Julia. *The Scout Mindset: Why Some People See Things Clearly and Others Don't*. Portfolio/Penguin, 2021.

Gallo, Carmine. *The Bezos Blueprint: Communication Secrets of the World's Greatest Salesman*. St. Martin's Press, 2022.

Gawdat, Mo. *Solve for Happy: Engineer Your Path to Joy*. North Star Way, 2017.

Godwin, Mark F. *Sapien Ethics: Who We Are, Why We Are Here, and How We Can Live Better*. Mark F. Godwin, 2021.

Gordon, Jon. *The Energy Bus: 10 Rules to Fuel Your Life, Work, and Team with Positive Energy*. John Wiley & Sons, 2007.

Gordon, Nachi, and Yisroel Besser, eds. *Meaningful Minute: Short Messages of Inspiration and Hope to Uplift and Illuminate Your Day*. Mesorah Publications, 2019.

Grant, Adam. *Originals: How Non-Conformists Move the World*. Penguin Books, 2017.

Grant, Adam. *Think Again: The Power of Knowing What You Don't Know*. Viking, 2021.

Grenville-Cleave, Bridget. *Positive Psychology: A Practical Guide*. MJF Books, 2012.

Haidt, Jonathan. *The Anxious Generation: How the Great Rewiring of Childhood Is Causing an Epidemic of Mental Illness*. Penguin Press, 2024.

Handy, Charles. *21 Letters on Life and Its Challenges*. Hutchinson, 2019.

Hawthorne, Emily Renk. *Of Mountains and Seas*. Hawk Ridge Press, 2024.

Heath, Chip and Dan. *The Power of Moments: Why Certain Experiences Have Extraordinary Impact*. Simon & Schuster, 2017.

Henion, Leigh Ann. *Phenomenal: A Hesitant Adventurer's Search for Wonder in the Natural World*. Penguin Books, 2015.

Holmes, Cassie. *Happier Hour: How to Beat Distraction, Expand Your Time, and Focus on What Matters Most*. Gallery Books, 2022.

Huang, Serena H. *The Inclusion Equation: Leveraging Data & AI for Organizational Diversity and Well-Being*. John Wiley & Sons, 2025.

Jackson, Laura Lynne. *Signs: The Secret Language of the Universe*. Dial Press, 2019.

Jackson, Matthew O. *The Human Network: How Your Social Position Determines Your Power, Beliefs, and Behaviors*. Pantheon, 2019.

Jardine, Lisa. *Worldly Goods: A New History of the Renaissance*. W. W. Norton, 1998.

Jiang, Ai. *A Palace Near the Wind: Natural Engines*. Titan Books, 2025.

Johnson, Stefanie K. *Inclusify: The Power of Uniqueness and Belonging to Build Innovative Teams*. Harper Business, 2020.

Kaag, John. *Sick Souls, Healthy Minds: How William James Can Save Your Life*. Princeton University Press, 2020.

Kaufman, Scott Barry, and Carolyn Gregoire. *Wired to Create: Unraveling the Mysteries of the Creative Mind*. TarcherPerigee, 2015.

Kem, Jen. *The Unicorn Team: The Nine Leadership Types You Need to Launch Your Big Ideas with Speed and Success*. Hay House, 2025.

Kinsley, Michael. *Old Age: A Beginner's Guide*. Tim Duggan Books, 2016.

Kishimi, Ichiro, and Fumitake Koga. *The Courage to Be Disliked: How to Free Yourself, Change Your Life, and Achieve Real Happiness*. Allen & Unwin, 2018.

Kline, Nancy. *Time to Think: Listening to Ignite the Human Mind*. Cassell Illustrated, 2021.

Koulopoulos, Thomas, and Dan Keldsen. *The Gen Z Effect: The Six Forces Shaping the Future of Business*. Taylor & Francis, 2014.

Kross, Ethan. *Chatter: The Voice in Our Head, Why It Matters, and How to Harness It*. Crown, 2021.

Kwik, Jim. *Limitless: Upgrade Your Brain, Learn Anything Faster, and Unlock Your Exceptional Life*. Expanded ed. Hay House, 2023.

Lakhiani, Vishen. *The Code of the Extraordinary Mind: 10 Unconventional Laws to Redefine Your Life and Succeed on Your Own Terms*. Rodale, 2016.

Lazarus, Doron. *Don't Mind if I Do: How to Transform your Life with the Power of Jewish Mindfulness*. CreateSpace, 2018.

Lee, Lorraine K. *Unforgettable Presence: Get Seen, Gain Influence, and Catapult Your Career*. John Wiley & Sons, 2025.

Lesher, Michael. *Miracles: The Extraordinary Life of Frieda Bassman*. Feldheim Publishers, 2017.

Levitin, Daniel J. *The Organized Mind: Thinking Straight in the Age of Information Overload*. Dutton, 2014.

Lichtenstein, Aharon. *By His Light: Character and Values in the Service of God*. Maggid, 2017.

Lickerman, Alex, and Ash ElDifrawi. *The Ten Worlds: The New Psychology of Happiness*. Health Communications, 2018.

Lin, Judy I. *Avatar Legends: City of Echoes*. Amulet Books, 2025.

List, John A. *The Voltage Effect: How to Make Good Ideas Great and Great Ideas Scale*.

Currency, 2022.

Lockwood, Georgene. *The Complete Idiot's Guide to Organizing Your Life*. 5th ed. Alpha Books, 2010.

Maimonides (Moses Ben Maimon). *Ethical Writings of Maimonides*. Edited by Raymond L. Weiss and Charles E. Butterworth. Dover Publications, 1975.

Milkman, Katy. *How to Change: The Science of Getting from Where You Are to Where You Want to Be*. Portfolio/Penguin, 2021.

Moawad, Trevor. *Getting to Neutral: How to Conquer Negativity and Thrive in a Chaotic World*. HarperOne, 2022.

Montoya, Peter. *The Brand Called You: The Ultimate Brand-Building and Business Development Handbook to Transform Anyone into an Indispensable Personal Brand*. Peter Montoya, 2005.

Morganstern, Julie. *Time Management from the Inside Out: The Foolproof System for Taking Control of Your Schedule—and Your Life*. Henry Holt, 2004.

Moriarty, Robin. *What Game Are You Playing? A Framework for Redefining Success and Achieving What Matters Most*. Greenleaf, 2019.

Morin, Amy. *13 Things Mentally Strong People Don't Do: Take Back Your Power, Embrace Change, Face Your Fears, and Train Your Brain for Happiness and Success*. HarperCollins, 2014.

Nessif, Bruna. *Let That Shit Go: A Journey to Forgiveness, Healing & Understanding Love*. CreateSpace, 2018.

Nez, Chester. *Code Talker: The First and Only Memoir by One of the Navajo Code Talkers of WW2*. Penguin, 2012.

Patterson, Carl. *Critical Thinking and Mental Models: The Great Course to Emulate Effective Thinking Systems of the Most Effective Leaders*. Independently Published, 2019.

Pemberton, Steve. *The Lighthouse Effect: How Ordinary People Can Have an Extraordinary Impact in the World*. Zondervan Books, 2021.

Perkel, Beth. *Light at the Beginning of the Tunnel: Wiring Our Children for Happiness*. Mosaica Press, 2021.

Peterson, Jordan B. *12 Rules for Life: An Antidote to Chaos*. Random House Canada, 2018.

Pink, Daniel H. *The Power of Regret: How Looking Backward Moves Us Forward*. Riverhead Books, 2022.

Price, Catherine. *The Power of Fun: How to Feel Alive Again*. Dial Press, 2021.

Rosenbaum, Elliott B. *The Valued Self: Five Steps to Healthy Self-Esteem*. iUniverse, 2011.

Schwarzman, Stephen A. *What It Takes: Lessons in the Pursuit of Excellence*. Avid Reader Press, 2019.

Seemiller, Corey, and Meghan Grace. *Generation Z Goes to College*. Jossey-Bass, 2016.

Seligman, Martin E. P. *Flourish: A Visionary New Understanding of Happiness and Well-Being*. Atria, 2011.

Sheldon, Kennon M., Todd B. Kashdan, and Michael F. Stegar, eds. *Designing Positive Psychology: Taking Stock and Moving Forward*. Oxford University Press, 2011.

Sockolov, Matthew. *Practicing Mindfulness: 75 Essential Meditations to Reduce Stress, Improve Mental Health, and Find Peace in the Everyday*. Althea Press, 2018.

Stillman, David and Jonah. *Gen Z @ Work: How the Next Generation Is Transforming the Workplace*. Harper Business, 2017.

Taleb, Nassim Nicholas. *The Black Swan: The Impact of the Highly Improbable*. 2nd ed. Random House, 2010.

Telford, Olivia. *Mastering the Art of Positive Thinking: Discovering the Joy in Every Moment*. Pristine, 2023.

Tippett, Krista. *Becoming Wise: An Inquiry into the Mystery and Art of Living*. Penguin Books, 2016.

Twenge, Jean M. *iGen: Why Today's Super-Connected Kids Are Growing Up Less Rebellious, More Tolerant, Less Happy—and Completely Unprepared for Adulthood*. Atria, 2017.

Vee, Julia, and Ken Bebelle. *Pearl City*. Tor, 2025.

Walsh, Justyn. *Investing with Keynes: How the World's Greatest Economist Overturned Conventional Wisdom and Made a Fortune on the Stock Market*. Pegasus Books, 2021.

Webb, Caroline. *How to Have a Good Day: Harness the Power of Behavioral Science to Transform Your Working Life*. Crown Business, 2016.

Weiner, Eric. *The Socrates Express: In Search of Life Lessons from Dead Philosophers*. Avid Reader Press, 2020.

WhispersRed, Emma. *Unwind Your Mind: The Life-Changing Power of ASMR*. HarperOne, 2019.

Wilber, Ken. *The Eye of Spirit: An Integral Vision for a World Gone Slightly Mad*. Shambhala, 2001.

Witt, Gregg L., and Derek E. Baird. *The Gen Z Frequency: How Brands Tune In & Build Credibility*. Kogan Page, 2018.

Zhu, Jenny Jing. *Dream Weaver: Finding Strength and Purpose in Life's Twists and Turns*. Indigo River, 2025.

Zimbardo, Philip, and John Boyd. *The Time Paradox: The New Psychology of Time That Will Change Your Life*. Free Press, 2008.

WEBSITES

Altagram. "How Different Generations Play Games." Accessed spring 2025. https://altagram
.com/gaming-of-different-generations.

Ball, Brinna Louise. "Marketing Video Games to Aging Demographics: A Generational Profile
Analysis." Master's thesis, Lindenwood University, March 2024. https://digitalcommons
.lindenwood.edu/cgi/viewcontent.cgi?article=1894&context=theses.

Beard, Alison, and Curt Nickisch, hosts. *HBR on Leadership*. Podcast. Accessed June 2025.
https://hbr.org/2023/05/podcast-hbr-on-leadership.

Bianchi, Giuliano. "Generation Z Work Ethic: Defending the Younger Working Generation."
EHL Insights. March 7, 2024. https://hospitalityinsights.ehl.edu/generation-z-work
-ethic-defending-younger-working-generation.

Blake, Suzanne. "Gen Z Is Done with Working from Home." *Newsweek*. March 1, 2024.
https://www.newsweek.com/gen-z-want-return-office-remote-work-1873924.

Brehe-Gunter, Emily. "1995 v. 2020: How College Admissions Has Changed over the Past 25
Years." KD College Prep. June 26, 2020. https://kdcollegeprep.com/how-college
-admissions-changed-last-25-years.

Clapp, Rob. "Two in Three Baby Boomers Now Gaming Due to COVID-19." WARC. Accessed
spring 2024. https://www.warc.com/content/paywall/article/warc-datapoints-gwi/two
-in-three-baby-boomers-now-gaming-due-to-covid-19/en-gb/133936?.

Costanzo, Greg. "Ask a Recruiter: How Long Does It Take to Land a Job Offer?" Columbia
SPS. July 2, 2020. https://sps.columbia.edu/news/ask-recruiter-how-long-does-it-take
-land-job-offer.

Crist, Carolyn. "Generation Z Employees Are More Willing to Bend the Rules to 'Get the Job
Done,' Survey Says." HR Dive. September 17, 2024. https://www.hrdive.com/news/gen-z
-employees-more-willing-to-bend-rules-workplace.

Deloitte. "2025 GenZ and Millennial Survey." Accessed 2025. https://www.deloitte.com
/global/en/issues/work/genz-millennial-survey.html.

Deloitte. "Millennials and Gen Z: Leading and Retaining Talent in the Multigenerational
Workplace." Accessed 2024. https://www2.deloitte.com/us/en/pages/about-deloitte
/articles/millennials-and-multigenerational-workplace.html.

De Witte, Melissa. "8 Ways Gen Z Will Change the Workforce." Stanford Report. February 14,
2024. https://news.stanford.edu/stories/2024/02/8-things-expect-gen-z-coworker.

Donelan, Chloe. "Gen Z in the Workplace: How Should Companies Adapt?" Johns Hopkins
University. April 18, 2023. https://imagine.jhu.edu/blog/2023/04/18/gen-z-in-the
-workplace-how-should-companies-adapt.

Dumas, Breck. "Gen Z Doesn't Trust Their Bosses to Give Career Advice—Here's What
They're Turning to Instead." *New York Post*. February 14, 2024. https://nypost
.com/2024/02/14/tech/gen-z-doesnt-trust-their-bosses-to-give-career-advice-heres-what

-theyre-turning-to-instead.

Enrich. "The Cost of Replacing an Employee and the Role of Financial Wellness." January 15, 2016. https://www.enrich.org/blog/The-true-cost-of-employee-turnover-financial -wellness-enrich.

Evans, Sophie. "Changing Lanes: Are Americans in Their Dream Career?" Moneypenny Resources. June 2023. https://www.moneypenny.com/us/resources/blog/changing-lanes -are-americans-in-their-dream-career-2.

Faber, Elizabeth. "Gen Zs and Millennials Seek Purpose and Progress in a Changing World: Insights from Deloitte's 2024 Gen Z and Millennial Survey." *Forbes.* May 15, 2024. https:// www.forbes.com/sites/deloitte/2024/05/15/gen-zs-and-millennials-seek-purpose-and -progress-in-a-changing-world-insights-from-deloittes-2024-gen-z-and-millennial -survey.

Greatest Generation. "The Greatest Generation Benefits Act Will Help American Seniors." July 22, 2023. https://thegreatestgen.org/the-greatest-generation-benefits-act-will-help -american-seniors.

Harmony Healthcare IT. "1 in 2 Gen Z with Anxiety Struggle Daily." October 7, 2023. https:// www.harmonyhit.com/gen-z-anxiety-statistics.

Hinkle, Amanda. "Job Hoppers: What Makes Gen Z Remain at a Job?" LinkedIn. March 20, 2024. https://www.linkedin.com/pulse/job-hoppers-what-makes-gen-z-remain-amanda -hinkle-vet5c.

INTOO. "INTOO Unlocking Organizational Success Report 2024." Accessed July 2024. https://www.intoo.com/uk/intoo-unlocking-organisational-success-report-2024.

Joblist. "2023 United States Job Market Trends Report." January 11, 2023. https://www.joblist .com/jobs-reports/2023-trends-united-states-job-market-report.

Jovanovska, Tamara. "The Gen Z Work Ethic Conundrum." Shortlister. Accessed March 2024. https://www.myshortlister.com/insights/gen-z-work-ethic.

Kaplan, Zoe. "'Problems' with Gen Z in the Workplace (From a Gen Zer)—and How to Fix Them." Forage. February 28, 2024. https://www.theforage.com/blog/basics/problems -gen-z-workplace.

Levine, Sean A. "Review of *Generations: The Real Differences Between Gen Z, Millennials, Gen X, Boomers, and Silents—and What They Mean for America's Future*, by Jean M. Twenge." *Chaplain Corps Journal.* May 1, 2024. https://www.lineofdeparture.army.mil/Journals /Military-Chaplaincy-Review/May-2024-Edition/Generations.

Lubrano, Alfred. "81% of Gen Z Believe They Can Write Self-Help Books." *The Union Democrat.* February 16, 2024. https://www.uniondemocrat.com/lifestyle /article_1bd8839a-ccf9-11ee-b03d-4380dff550f8.html.

Masterson, Danielle. "How Baby Boomers Are Shaping the Gaming Segment." NutraIngredients USA. April 21, 2022. https://www.nutraingredients-usa.com /Article/2022/04/21/How-baby-boomers-are-shaping-the-gaming-segment.

McAllister, Sean. "How Is Gen Z Changing the Workplace?" Zurich. May 23, 2025. https://www.zurich.com/media/magazine/2022/how-will-gen-z-change-the-future-of-work.

Meehan, Orla. "New Free Report: How and Why Different Generations Engage with Video Games in 2023." Newzoo. November 8, 2023. https://newzoo.com/resources/blog/how-and-why-different-generations-engage-with-video-games-in-2023.

Milojevic, Natasa. "The Gen Z Effect and the Workforce Evolution: 2024 Statistics." Cake.com. Accessed spring 2024. https://cake.com/empowered-team/gen-z-workforce-statistics.

Murphy, Almha. "Is the Gen Z Work Ethic Different?" April 9, 2024. https://www.businessbecause.com/news/insights/9301/gen-z-work-ethic.

Parmelee, Michele. "Making Waves: How Gen Z and Millennials Are Prioritizing—and Driving—Change in the Workplace." Deloitte Insights. May 17, 2023. https://www2.deloitte.com/us/en/insights/topics/talent/recruiting-gen-z-and-millennials.html.

Phelan, Julia. "Onboarding New Employees—Without Overwhelming Them." *Harvard Business Review*. April 2, 2024. https://hbr.org/2024/04/onboarding-new-employees-without-overwhelming-them.

Qualtrics. "Qualtrics Announces Top Employee Trends for 2024." PR Newswire. October 25, 2023. https://www.prnewswire.com/news-releases/qualtrics-announces-top-employee-trends-for-2024-301966899.html.

Rael, Hannah. "Number of U.S. Public High School Students Guaranteed to Take a Personal Finance Course on Track to Double to 53% by 2030." Next Gen Personal Finance. April 15, 2024. https://www.ngpf.org/blog/press-releases/number-of-us-public-high-school-students-guaranteed-to-take-a-personal-finance-course-on-track-to-double-to-53-by-2030.

Richard, Ang. "Generation Z in the Workplace." National Association of Colleges and Employees. January 16, 2024. https://www.naceweb.org/talent-acquisition/student-attitudes/generation-z-in-the-workplace.

Richmond, Jason. "Gen Z in the Workforce: Challenging or Change-Makers?" *Forbes*. January 23, 2024. https://www.forbes.com/councils/forbesbusinesscouncil/2024/01/23/gen-z-in-the-workforce-challenging-or-change-makers.

Sales Education Foundation. "Key Statistics on Professional Sales Education." 2023. https://salesfoundation.org/wp-content/uploads/2024/07/2023-key-stats-sales-education.pdf.

Sheldon, Ashly Moore. "Tales from the Self-Help Shelves." ThriftBooks. December 17, 2023. https://www.thriftbooks.com/blog/tales-from-the-self-help-shelves.

Staglin, Garen. "The Future of Work Depends on Supporting Gen Z." *Forbes*. August 29, 2022. https://www.forbes.com/sites/onemind/2022/07/22/the-future-of-work-depends-on-supporting-gen-z.

Statista. "Distribution of Video Gamers in the United States in 2023, by Generation." Accessed January 2025. https://www.statista.com/statistics/189582/age-of-us-video-game-players.

Stern, Caryl M. "Generation Z Is Waging a Battle Against Depression, Addiction and Hopelessness." Walton Family Foundation. September 8, 2022. https://www .waltonfamilyfoundation.org/stories/foundation/generation-z-is-waging-a-battle-against -depression-addiction-and-hopelessness.

SWNS. "Gen Z Confident They Could Write a Better Self-Help Book Than Millennials, Boomers." *New York Post*. December 20, 2023. https://nypost.com/2023/12/20/lifestyle /gen-z-more-confident-they-could-offer-better-life-advice-than-millennials-boomers.

Tello, Cynthia. "Review of *Generations: The Real Differences Between Gen Z, Millennials, Gen X, Boomers, and Silents—and What They Mean for America's Future*, by Jean M. Twenge." *QRCA Views*, June 12, 2024. https://www.qrcaviews.org/2024/06/12/generations-the -real-differences-between-gen-z-millennials-gen-x-boomers-and-silents-and-what-they -mean-for-americas-future-by-jean-m-twenge-atria-books-2023.

Twenge, Jean M. "Gen Z Really Does Have a Work Ethic Problem." Generation Tech. November 15, 2023. https://www.generationtechblog.com/p/gen-z-really-does-have-a -work-ethic.

Voicu, Ana. "How Gen Z Is Changing the Workplace." January 13, 2025. https://www.wework .com/ideas/workspace-solutions/how-gen-z-is-changing-the-workplace.

Way, Wendy L., and Karen Holden. "Teachers' Background and Capacity to Teach Personal Finance: Results of a National Study." National Endowment for Financial Education. 2010. https://www.fdic.gov/about/advisory-committees/economic-inclusion/2011/mar3 .pdf.

Workable. "The Great Divide: 4 Things About Gen Z's Work Ethic You Probably Didn't Know." January 2025. https://resources.workable.com/inside-hr/stories-and-insights/gen-z -work-ethic.

Zhou, Danjing. "Insights into Baby Boomer Gamers." Newzoo. October 6, 2021. https:// newzoo.com/resources/blog/insights-into-baby-boomer-gamers.

ZipRecruiter. "Entry Level College Grads Salary." Accessed spring 2024. https://www .ziprecruiter.com/Salaries/Entry-Level-College-Grads-Salary.

ABOUT THE AUTHOR

Kat Walsh is a writer, keynote speaker, consultant, and Gen Z-ologist who has spent years researching and advising executive leaders across all industries to help them attract, integrate, and develop Gen Z in their workplaces. With a background in conflict resolution and future-focused leadership, she has coached and advised executive leadership teams from Fortune 500 companies to start-ups and first-time managers on how to turn young professionals into high-performing leaders.

Known for her ability to guide complex, nondisruptive transformation, Kat focuses on operational effectiveness, leadership development, and profitable performance across the organization. She's also a frequent guest lecturer on the news, in podcasts, and at universities, and she serves as an advisor at the University of Chicago's Polsky Center for Entrepreneurship and Innovation. Kat lives in the Chicago area and is the mother of four, three of whom are Gen Z.

www.ingramcontent.com/pod-product-compliance
Lightning Source LLC
Chambersburg PA
CBHW021929190326
41519CB00009B/960